DATE DUE

DEMCO, INC. 38-2931

THE MIDDLE EAST

O P P O S I N G V I E W P O I N T S ®

Other Books of Related Interest

THE MIDDLE EAST

O P P O S I N G   V I E W P O I N T S ®

William Dudley, *Book Editor*

Daniel Leone, *President*
Bonnie Szumski, *Publisher*
Scott Barbour, *Managing Editor*
Helen Cothran, *Senior Editor*

OPPOSING
VIEWPOINTS®
SERIES

GREENHAVEN
PRESS®

THOMSON
━━━━━★━━━━━ ™
GALE

San Diego • Detroit • New York • San Francisco • Cleveland
New Haven, Conn. • Waterville, Maine • London • Munich

Cover credit: AP/Wide World Photos

LIBRARY OF CONGRESS CATALOGING-IN-PUBLICATION DATA

The Middle East / William Dudley, book editor.
  p. cm. — (Opposing viewpoints series)
  Includes bibliographical references and index.
  ISBN 0-7377-1806-4 (pbk. : alk. paper) — ISBN 0-7377-1805-6 (lib. : alk. paper)
    1. Ethnic conflict—Middle East. 2. Arab-Israeli conflict. 3. Islam and politics—Middle East. 4. Violence—Religious aspects—Islam. 5. Peace—Religious aspects—Islam. 6. Middle East—Foreign relations—United States. 7. United States—Foreign relations—Middle East. I. Dudley, William. II. Series.
  HM1121.M53 2004
  305.8'00956—dc21   2003049020

Printed in the United States of America

"Congress shall make
no law. . . abridging the
freedom of speech, or of
the press."

First Amendment to the U.S. Constitution

The basic foundation of our democracy is the First
Amendment guarantee of freedom of expression.
The Opposing Viewpoints Series is dedicated to the
concept of this basic freedom and the idea that it is
more important to practice it than to enshrine it.

Contents

Why Consider
Opposing Viewpoints?

"The only way in which a human being can make some approach to knowing the whole of a subject is by hearing what can be said about it by persons of every variety of opinion and studying all modes in which it can be looked at by every character of mind. No wise man ever acquired his wisdom in any mode but this."

John Stuart Mill

In our media-intensive culture it is not difficult to find differing opinions. Thousands of newspapers and magazines and dozens of radio and television talk shows resound with differing points of view. The difficulty lies in deciding which opinion to agree with and which "experts" seem the most credible. The more inundated we become with differing opinions and claims, the more essential it is to hone critical reading and thinking skills to evaluate these ideas. Opposing Viewpoints books address this problem directly by presenting stimulating debates that can be used to enhance and teach these skills. The varied opinions contained in each book examine many different aspects of a single issue. While examining these conveniently edited opposing views, readers can develop critical thinking skills such as the ability to compare and contrast authors' credibility, facts, argumentation styles, use of persuasive techniques, and other stylistic tools. In short, the Opposing Viewpoints Series is an ideal way to attain the higher-level thinking and reading skills so essential in a culture of diverse and contradictory opinions.

In addition to providing a tool for critical thinking, Opposing Viewpoints books challenge readers to question their own strongly held opinions and assumptions. Most people form their opinions on the basis of upbringing, peer pressure, and personal, cultural, or professional bias. By reading carefully balanced opposing views, readers must directly confront new ideas as well as the opinions of those with whom they disagree. This is not to simplistically argue that everyone who reads opposing views will—or should—change his or her opinion. Instead, the series enhances readers' understanding of their own views by encouraging confrontation with opposing ideas. Careful examination of others' views can lead to the readers' understanding of the logical inconsistencies in their own opinions, perspective on why they hold an opinion, and the consideration of the possibility that their opinion requires further evaluation.

Evaluating Other Opinions

To ensure that this type of examination occurs, Opposing Viewpoints books present all types of opinions. Prominent spokespeople on different sides of each issue as well as well-known professionals from many disciplines challenge the reader. An additional goal of the series is to provide a forum for other, less known, or even unpopular viewpoints. The opinion of an ordinary person who has had to make the decision to cut off life support from a terminally ill relative, for example, may be just as valuable and provide just as much insight as a medical ethicist's professional opinion. The editors have two additional purposes in including these less known views. One, the editors encourage readers to respect others' opinions—even when not enhanced by professional credibility. It is only by reading or listening to and objectively evaluating others' ideas that one can determine whether they are worthy of consideration. Two, the inclusion of such viewpoints encourages the important critical thinking skill of objectively evaluating an author's credentials and bias. This evaluation will illuminate an author's reasons for taking a particular stance on an issue and will aid in readers' evaluation of the author's ideas.

It is our hope that these books will give readers a deeper understanding of the issues debated and an appreciation of the complexity of even seemingly simple issues when good and honest people disagree. This awareness is particularly important in a democratic society such as ours in which people enter into public debate to determine the common good. Those with whom one disagrees should not be regarded as enemies but rather as people whose views deserve careful examination and may shed light on one's own.

Thomas Jefferson once said that "difference of opinion leads to inquiry, and inquiry to truth." Jefferson, a broadly educated man, argued that "if a nation expects to be ignorant and free . . . it expects what never was and never will be." As individuals and as a nation, it is imperative that we consider the opinions of others and examine them with skill and discernment. The Opposing Viewpoints Series is intended to help readers achieve this goal.

David L. Bender and Bruno Leone,
Founders

Greenhaven Press anthologies primarily consist of previously published material taken from a variety of sources, including periodicals, books, scholarly journals, newspapers, government documents, and position papers from private and public organizations. These original sources are often edited for length and to ensure their accessibility for a young adult audience. The anthology editors also change the original titles of these works in order to clearly present the main thesis of each viewpoint and to explicitly indicate the opinion presented in the viewpoint. These alterations are made in consideration of both the reading and comprehension levels of a young adult audience. Every effort is made to ensure that Greenhaven Press accurately reflects the original intent of the authors included in this anthology.

Introduction

"The Middle East has often been left behind in the political and economic advancement of the world. That is the history of the region. But it need not and must not be its fate."

— *President George W. Bush, April 4, 2002.*

The *Middle East*, a term first used in a 1902 article by American naval historian Alfred Thayer Mahan, refers to a geographic region of southwestern Asia that also includes parts of northern Africa and southeastern Europe. Although there is some scholarly disagreement on exactly which countries are part of the Middle East, one generally accepted definition includes the countries of Bahrain, Egypt, Iran, Iraq, Israel, Jordan, Kuwait, Lebanon, Oman, Qatar, Saudi Arabia, Sudan, Syria, Turkey, United Arab Emirates, and Yemen. These countries cover an area of approximately 3.7 million square miles and are home to a population of about 350 million people. Situated between three continents, the region has been the site of human civilization for more than five thousand years.

Unfortunately, the region's recent history has been most notable for its political instability, conflict, and war. The endemic political violence occurring in the area in the twentieth century has carried over into the twenty-first; in March 2003, for example, an invasion force consisting of American and British forces entered the Middle Eastern nation of Iraq. The stated goal of the invasion was to forcibly end the regime of Saddam Hussein, president of Iraq since 1979. Hussein, who had previously involved his country in war when he attacked Iran in 1980 and Kuwait in 1990, had been accused of threatening American and world security by developing weapons of mass destruction and supporting terrorist groups. U.S. president George W. Bush and others feared that terrorists, assisted by Iraq, would attack the United States with such weapons.

Both before and after the commencement of war, however, various Bush administration officials, including the president himself, voiced the hope that the invasion could have beneficial changes in addition to Iraqi disarmament. They predicted that a successful U.S.-instigated "regime change" in Iraq could result in the creation of a democratic government there, much as Germany and Japan became democracies following World War II. Some even ventured to predict that such a development would in turn inspire democratic reforms throughout the Middle East. Most of the countries in the region are ruled by authoritarian governments in which dissent is suppressed and people have little say in how they are governed—a situation that has persisted despite the post–Cold War wave of democracy that transformed much of Europe, Africa, and South America in the 1980s and 1990s. But, as President Bush stated in a February 2003 speech, "a new regime in Iraq would serve as a dramatic and inspiring example of freedom for other nations in the region. It is presumptuous and insulting to suggest that a whole region of the world . . . is somehow untouched by the most basic aspirations of life." Bush and his supporters have held out the possibility that American military power, coupled with the democratic aspirations of the peoples of the region, might give birth to a new political era for the Middle East.

The American and British military effort to oust Saddam Hussein in 2003 was a quick success; within a month the regime was finished and American troops were met by cheering crowds in the Iraqi capital of Baghdad. Whether or not Bush's broader vision of Middle East democratization is realizable is a matter of debate. Indeed, much in the region's troubled history seems to argue against success. The creation of Iraq and its neighbors was itself the product of a war involving foreign powers. In World War I (1914–1918) the Turkish Ottoman Empire, which had ruled most of the Middle East since the 1500s, collapsed. The empire's demise set the stage for the genesis of new states that constitute the present-day map of the region—a genesis that was aided and abetted by the victorious World War I nations, especially Great Britain and France. The two nations divided much of the region between them and fostered the creation of states to protect their interests. Iraq, for example, was cobbled together by the British from three Ottoman provinces populated by an amalgam of peoples, including ethnic Kurds, Shiite Arabs, and Sunni Arabs.

Creating democratic sovereign nations was not the goal of the French and British after World War I. They instead wanted stable regimes whose governments would protect British and French interests. To that end, for example, Great Britain created a monarchy in Iraq and arranged for the accession of an Arab tribal leader (and World War I ally) to rule Iraq as King Faisal. The discovery of oil in large quantities in the Middle East during the 1920s and 1930s added to foreign interest in the region. Following World War II the United States and the Soviet Union replaced Great Britain and France as the leading foreign powers in the Middle East. During the long Cold War (1945–1989), both superpowers courted governments, built alliances, and protected arrangements for oil exploration and development; neither was overly concerned about creating democracies in the region.

The attempts by Great Britain and other countries to cre-

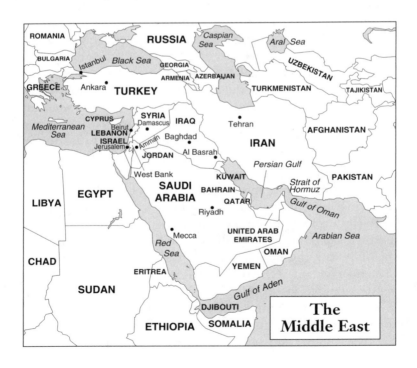

14

ate and manage Middle East nations is one reason, many believe, for the region's history of violence. For much of the twentieth century the people of the Middle East have struggled in various ways against foreign control. Opposition to foreign intervention in the Middle East has taken several forms. As early as 1920 the people of Iraq revolted against British rule and were forcibly suppressed. In the 1950s and 1960s, Arab nationalism was an important force. A new generation of military officers took over the governments of many Arab states, in some cases violently overthrowing governments that had cooperated with Great Britain and France. King Faisal II of Iraq was deposed and killed in 1958, for example, and replaced by a series of military dictators that culminated with Saddam Hussein. Arab nationalism was also directed at Israel, a nation founded in 1948 as a homeland for Jews. Many Arab leaders condemned Israel's Jewish emigrants from Europe and other places as alien invaders and viewed Israel's creation as something forced on them by the United States and other outside powers. A coalition of Arab nations immediately attacked Israel in 1948 in what was to be the first of several wars between Israel and its neighbors.

In the 1970s and later, Middle East resistance to foreign and American influence became more explicitly religious in nature. The religion of Islam, which has been inextricably linked to the region's society and culture for hundreds of years, emerged as a strong political force in many Middle East countries, in some cases superseding Arab nationalism. For example, Muslims demanded more political power in Lebanon's government, leading to civil war and conflict in that country in the 1970s and 1980s that in turn caused Lebanon's neighbors, Syria and Israel, to intervene militarily. In 1979 Muslim religious leader Ayatollah Ruhollah Khomeini successfully led a revolution that toppled Iran's U.S.-supported government. In addition, Islamic-sponsored terrorist groups based in the Middle East have engaged in numerous acts of terrorism against Israel, and more recently, the United States—including the September 11, 2001, attacks.

As many commentators have pointed out, the region's history of resistance to foreign designs may complicate, if not prevent, American efforts to spread democracy in the Middle East, despite America's initial military success in the 2003 Iraq war. "Such grandiose visions," writes political columnist Walter Shapiro, "are fraught with danger if . . . we ignore the sway of nationalism and historical memory." Historian Mark Mazower argues that "American troops would have to remain in the region for a very long time" for any realistic chance at creating a democratic and pro-American government in Iraq. But the longer they stay, he points out, the more likely they will be viewed as an unwelcome foreign (and non-Muslim) occupation force rather than as democratic liberators. Even if the United States were to succeed in helping Iraq create a functioning democratic regime, many observers believe that other Middle East nations may view Iraq not as a model to emulate, but as a weak victim of foreign conquest. As a team of scholars from the Carnegie Endowment for International Peace puts it, the idea that people in the region "would respond to the establishment of a U.S.-installed, nominally democratic Iraqi regime by rising up in a surge of pro-democratic protests, . . . and installing pro-western, pluralist regimes is far-fetched."

The political future of the Middle East is one of several key questions debated in *The Middle East: Opposing Viewpoints* in the following chapters: Why Is the Middle East a Conflict Area? How Does Islam Affect the Middle East? What Role Should the United States Play in the Middle East? Is Peace Between Israel and the Palestinians Possible? The wide-ranging viewpoints in this volume can help readers better understand some of the issues facing the Middle East and gain insight into whether a lasting peace in the region can be achieved.

CHAPTER 1

Why Is the Middle East a Conflict Area?

Chapter Preface

The Middle East has long been a center of ethnic, religious, and political rivalries. One issue that illustrates the persistent nature of these conflicts is the Arab-Israeli dispute. After World War I, Palestine, a former province of the Turkish Ottoman Empire, came under British administrative rule. At this time, Palestine was primarily populated by Arabs—both Muslims and Christians—and by Jews, who comprised 10 percent of the population. The number of Jews in Palestine increased, however, after World War II, during which 6 million European Jews were killed in the Nazi Holocaust. This calamity bolstered efforts on the part of Zionists to establish a Jewish homeland in Palestine. Responding in part to Zionist demands, the United Nations in 1947 voted to divide Palestine into Jewish and Arab states—a decision that was rejected by neighboring Arab nations. Jewish nationalists proclaimed the establishment of the state of Israel in 1948, accepting the boundaries delineated by the UN resolution. The armies of Egypt, Iraq, Jordan, and Lebanon immediately invaded Israel, but were defeated in 1949.

Subsequent wars between Arab nations and Israel erupted in 1956, 1967, 1973, and 1982. In addition, in 1987, 1996, and 2000 widespread civil violence broke out within Israel between Israelis and Palestinians—violence that has continued to this day. Much of this conflict concerns the large number of Palestinian refugees displaced when Israel was formed. After 1948 large numbers of Palestinians—some uprooted by war, some fearing for their safety in a new Jewish state, and some trying to escape extremist groups on both sides—fled Israel. Most of these refugees—and their descendants—are now living in camps in the West Bank and the Gaza Strip, territories that Israel has occupied since the 1967 Six-Day War. Palestinian demands for Israel to give up these lands to Palestinian control, and Israeli efforts to protect Israel from Palestinian militant violence, are a continuing source of friction in the region.

The Arab-Israeli dispute is not the only cause of conflict in the Middle East, of course. The region's role as a vital supplier of oil increases its potential for political, territorial, and economic strife as nations vie for control over this precious resource. Iraq's 1990 invasion of Kuwait, for example, was largely seen as motivated by Iraq's desire to obtain its neighbor's vast petroleum resources. Prior to that, territorial and religious animosities between Iraq and Iran erupted into the region's bloodiest twentieth-century war, which lasted from 1980 to 1988 and resulted in more than 1 million casualties. The causes of such wars and conflict in the region are analyzed in the following chapter.

"In the long-run, the only hope for a normal, peaceful life for the people of Israel is for their government to end their occupation of Palestinian land."

Israeli Occupation of Palestinian Lands Is a Source of Conflict

A Jewish Voice for Peace

Many observers have argued that a key cause of conflict in the Middle East has been Israel's occupation of territories it conquered in the 1967 war. These territories include the West Bank (formerly held by Jordan), Gaza and the Sinai Peninsula (held by Egypt) and the Golan Heights (held by Syria). Israel signed a peace agreement with Egypt in 1978 and returned Sinai in 1982, annexed the Golan Heights in 1981, and allowed some Palestinian self-rule in parts of the remaining occupied territories in Gaza and the West Bank in the 1990s. In the following viewpoint by A Jewish Voice for Peace, the authors contend that violence will be inevitable in the Middle East as long as Israel continues to occupy Palestinian territory. They contend that Israel's occupation brutalizes Palestinians, is condemned by the world, and is unnecessary for Israel's security. A Jewish Voice for Peace is a California-based activist organization.

As you read, consider the following questions:

1. Why are Jewish settlements in territories outside Israel's 1967 boundaries illegal, according to the authors?
2. What human rights violations against the Palestinian people do the authors describe and condemn?

A Jewish Voice for Peace, *From Jew to Jew: Why We Should Oppose the Israeli Occupation of the West Bank and Gaza*. Berkeley, CA: A Jewish Voice for Peace, 2002. Copyright © 2002 by A Jewish Voice for Peace. Reproduced by permission.

B ased in the San Francisco Bay Area, A JEWISH VOICE FOR PEACE is the oldest and largest of a growing number of Jewish groups that are convinced that the Israeli occupation of Palestinian territory must end. There are two compelling reasons for this. First, we wish to preserve the best part of our Jewish heritage—a deeply-ingrained sense of morality—and pass it on to the next generation, unsullied by the mistreatment of another people. We were brought up to believe that, as Jews, we are obligated to always take the moral high road and we can't imagine letting this proud ethical tradition die now.

Second, we are convinced that the only way to ensure the security of the people of Israel is for their government to conclude a just peace with the Palestinians. Without some reasonable version of justice being done, there will never be peace, and so we oppose any Israeli government policy that denies the Palestinians their legitimate rights. . . .

In the interest of peace, and with an open heart and mind, please consider the following facts.

1. The Occupation

The international community, through the United Nations and other forums, has made it clear that virtually the entire world considers the Israeli occupation of territories it captured in the 1967 war to be wrong and contrary to basic principles of international law. Every year since 1967 (up until the Oslo Process started [in 1993]), the UN General Assembly passed the same resolution (usually by lopsided votes like 150-2), stating that Israel is obligated to vacate the West Bank, Gaza and East Jerusalem, in exchange for security guaranteed by the international community, in accordance with UN Resolution 242.

While the circumstances were much different, the legal basis of these resolutions is the same principle used to force Iraq out of Kuwait [in 1991]—i.e., a country cannot annex or indefinitely occupy territory gained by force of arms. The only reason that Israel is able to maintain its occupation of Palestinian land is that the US routinely vetoes every Security Council resolution that would insist that Israel live up to its obligations under international law.

One of the original goals of Zionism was to create a Jewish state that would be just another normal country. If that is what Israel wants (and that is a reasonable goal), then it must be held to the same standards as any other country, including the prohibition against annexing territory captured by force of arms.

2. The Settlements

Similarly, all Jewish settlements, every single one, in territories outside Israel's 1967 boundaries, are a direct violation of the Geneva Conventions, which Israel has signed and is obligated to abide by, as well as UN Security Council Resolutions 446 and 465. As John Quigley, a professor of international law at Ohio State has written, "The Geneva Convention requires an occupying power to change the existing order as little as possible during its tenure. One aspect of this obligation is that it must leave the territory to the people it finds there. It may not bring its own people to populate the country. This prohibition is found in the convention's Article 49 which states, 'The Occupying Power shall not deport or transfer parts of its own civilian population into the territory it occupies.'". . .

In fact, on December 5, 2001, Switzerland convened a conference of 114 nations that have signed the Fourth Geneva Convention (a conference boycotted by the US and Israel). The assembled nations decided *unanimously* that the Convention did indeed apply to the occupied territories, that Israel was in gross violation of their obligations under that Convention, that Jewish-only settlements in those territories were illegal under the rules of the Convention, and that it was the responsibility of the other contracting parties to stop these violations of international law.

To be in such flagrant violation of the norms of international behavior is bad for Israel's standing in the world, bad for the Jewish people as a whole and, as we shall see, totally unnecessary.

3. Israel's Security

It is sometimes argued that the settlements are necessary for Israel's security, to protect Israel from terrorism and the threat of violence. But the reality is that the settlements are a major cause of Israel's current security problems, not the cure for them. *New York Times* columnist Anthony Lewis pointed out the aggressive nature of the settlements as follows, "It is false to see the settlements as ordinary villages or towns where Israelis only want to live in peace with their Palestinian neighbors. They are in fact imposed by force—superior Israeli military force—on Palestinian territory. Many have been built precisely to assert Israeli power and ownership. They are not peaceful villages but militarized encampments . . . The settlement policy is not just a political but a moral danger to the character of the state."

Palestinian Actions

"But wouldn't the Palestinians use their own state as a base for even more attacks against Israel?", it might be asked. For one, the Palestinians have long agreed that their future state would be non-militarized, no foreign forces hostile to Israel would be allowed in, and international monitors could be stationed on Palestinian land in order to verify these conditions.

Terrorism and Hope

As for individual acts of terrorism, there is an historical precedent that gives a realistic answer to this question. During the first years after the Oslo agreements were signed [in 1993], Hamas[1] tried to disrupt the peace process but, because of the prevailing optimism, their influence in Palestinian society diminished and their armed attacks fell off sharply. What that means for the future is that if the Palestinian people feel that even a rough version of justice has been done, they will not support the more extreme elements in their political spectrum. This is not just guesswork; it already happened with just the hope of justice being done.

Another aspect of this is that if Israel had internationally recognized borders, then they could be defended much more easily than the current situation where every hill in Palestine is a potential bone of contention because of Jewish settlements encroaching on Palestinian land. If they and their settlers and the military apparatus they require were gone, and the Palestinians were given enough aid by the in-

---

1. Hamas is a militant Palestinian group, formed in 1987, that seeks to replace Israel with an Islamic Palestinian state. Hamas has been classified as a terrorist organization by the United States.

ternational community to create a viable economy in their own state, they would naturally be overjoyed and a positive turn of events would be the inevitable result.

4. *"But Don't They Just Want to Drive the Jews into the Sea?"*

Officially since 1988, and unofficially for years before that, the Palestinian position has been that they recognize Israel's right to exist in peace and security within their 1967 borders. Period. At the same time, they expect to be allowed to establish a truly independent, viable, contiguous, non-militarized state in all of the West Bank, Gaza and East Jerusalem. This is what UN Resolution 242 says: "Land for Peace"—and the Palestinian Authority has stated repeatedly that UN Resolution 242 has to be the basis for any long-lasting solution to the conflict.

It is true that some Palestinians advocate that all of historic Palestine should be under Arab control, but there is no support for this position, either in the international community, nor among most Palestinians. Statements to that effect are just hyperbole and do not represent the official Palestinian position. Similarly, statements by some Palestinians inciting people to violence against Israelis can easily be matched by statements from Orthodox rabbis and fundamentalist settlers calling for death to the Arabs. There are *meshuganahs* [crazy people] aplenty on both sides.

But since the Palestinians' official position is clear, why shouldn't Israel take the Palestinians up on this offer and withdraw from the occupied territories? Israel is far stronger militarily than all the Arab armies combined and would face no credible military threat from a Palestinian state. And the threat of individual terrorist acts would, of necessity, be much less once the Palestinians felt that they had received a modicum of justice.

What would Israel lose by this obvious solution of just ending the occupation, which they could do tomorrow if they wanted to (or if the US insisted that they do so)? The only thing it would "lose" is the dream of some of its citizens for a "Greater Israel", where Israel's boundaries are expanded to its biblical borders. The problem with that dream is that it totally ignores the legitimate rights of the Palestinian people, and the will of virtually the entire international community. As long as the right-wing settlers and their supporters in the Israeli government insist on pursuing this dream, there will be nothing but bloodshed forever. The Palestinian people have lived in Palestine for thousands of years and they are not going away. Israel must conclude a just peace with them or innocent blood will continue to be shed indefinitely.

5. Negotiations Leading up to the Current Intifada

It has often been asked, "But didn't [Israeli prime minister Ehud] Barak offer 95% of the Occupied Territories to [Palestinian leader Yassar] Arafat at Camp David [in 2000] and

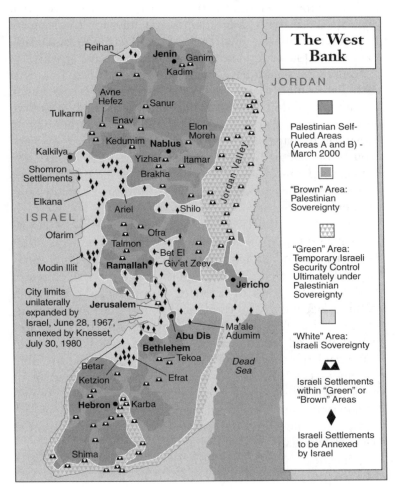

The West Bank

JORDAN

Palestinian Self-Ruled Areas (Areas A and B) - March 2000

"Brown" Area: Palestinian Sovereignty

"Green" Area: Temporary Israeli Security Control Ultimately under Palestinian Sovereignty

"White" Area: Israeli Sovereignty

Israeli Settlements within "Green" or "Brown" Areas

Israeli Settlements to be Annexed by Israel

doesn't his rejection of that offer mean that they don't want peace?" There are several crucial things to understand here. First, prisoners may occupy 95% of a prison's space, but it is the other 5% that determines who is in control. Similarly, the offer Barak made at Camp David II would have left the main settlement blocks and their Jewish-only bypass roads in place. Along with the extensive areas Israel planned on retaining indefinitely for its military use, this would have dissected Palestinian territory into separate bantustans ("native reservations"), isolated from each other, each surrounded by Israeli-controlled territory, having no common borders with each other or other Arab nations, with no control over their own air-space, with their main water aquifers (underneath the settlement blocs) taken by Israel, and with the Israeli military able to surround and blockade each enclave at will.

Jerusalem would have been similarly dissected so that each Palestinian island would be surrounded by an Israeli sea. This wouldn't be an acceptable "end of the conflict" to you if you were Palestinian, would it? Please see the map on [the previous page] and see for yourself what this "most generous" offer actually looked like. (Israel actually presented no maps at Camp David itself, but this was their offer of two months previous, and only marginal additional territory was theoretically offered at Camp David.)

The other important question here is 95% of what? "Greater Jerusalem" was unilaterally annexed by Israel after the 1967 war and so it was not included as West Bank territory in Barak's offer, even though it takes up a large chunk of the West Bank, most of it having no municipal connection with the actual city of Jerusalem. The international community has never recognized Israeli sovereignty over "Greater Jerusalem" and has repeatedly declared that Israel should withdraw from this and all territories it conquered by force of arms in 1967. Barak's offer also excluded large swaths of the Jordan Valley which the Israeli military would control indefinitely. Thus the Foundation for Middle East Peace estimates that the actual percentage of occupied land offered to the Palestinians was more like 80%, not 95%. . . .

6. Looking at Cause and Effect

"What about Palestinian crimes? Why don't you lay equal

blame on them?" Certainly, Palestinians have committed grave crimes, and in any process of reconciliation, both sides will have much to answer for. But as Jews, we are responsible to look at Israel objectively, and not just when Israelis are victims of violence.

Must Understand History

In order to understand why there is the level of violence we see today, it is necessary to understand how we got to this point.

a) Before the 1967 war. Before the Israeli occupation of the West Bank and Gaza, there was little organized Palestinian resistance. The majority of the tension was between Israel and the neighboring states. For the most part, violence between Israel and the Palestinians was limited to isolated Palestinian "infiltrations", as Israel generally referred to them.

The Israeli population may certainly have believed that they were in mortal danger from the armies of their Arab neighbors. But by the mid-1960s, Israeli leaders had a good deal of confidence that they could defeat a combination of Arab forces similar to that which they acomplished in 1948, and with greater ease. History, of course, proved them correct, which calls into question the myth that Israel was fighting a self-defensive war for its very existence in 1967.

The 1967 War

b) The 1967 war itself. The myth that the 1967 war was a purely defensive one is further weakened by statements of Israeli leaders themselves. For example, the *New York Times* published an article on May 11, 1997 quoting Moshe Dayan's[2] own diaries, in which he admits that the kibbutz residents who pressed the Government to take the Golan Heights in 1967 did so less for security than for the farmland. "They didn't even try to hide their greed for that land . . . The Syrians, on the fourth day of the war, were not a threat to us", Dayan wrote.

Or again from Professor John Quigley's landmark book, *Palestine And Israel*, "Mordecai Bentov, a cabinet minister who attended the June 4 (1967) cabinet meeting and sup-

2. Moshe Dayan was Israel's defense minister during the 1967 war.

ported the decision to invade Egypt, said Israel's 'entire story' about 'the danger of extermination' was 'invented of whole cloth and exaggerated after the fact to justify the annexation of new Arab territories'."

Even Menachem Begin[3] said, "The Egyptian army concentrations in the Sinai approaches do not prove that [Egyptian leader Gamal Abdel] Nasser was really about to attack us. We must be honest with ourselves. We decided to attack him." In short, the argument of self-defense does not stand up to a close examination of the historical record.

c) Peace Proposals after the 1967 war. In 1969, [Richard] Nixon's Secretary of State, William Rogers, proposed a peace plan based on UN Resolution 242, which would have guaranteed Israel's security within her pre-1967 borders. Israel rejected it out-of-hand. In 1971, Egyptian President Anwar Sadat offered Israel a similar proposal (which did not mention Palestinian rights at all). This was also rejected by Israel.

In 1976, Egypt, Syria, Jordan and the PLO [Palestine Liberation Organization] supported a resolution in the UN Security Council affirming Israel's right to exist in peace and security, as in UN Resolution 242, but with a Palestinian state created alongside Israel. Israel opposed it and the US vetoed it. Arafat personally reaffirmed his support of a two-state solution in statements made to Senator Adlai Stevenson in 1976, and Representative Paul Findley and *New York Times* columnist Anthony Lewis in 1978. The Saudis made similar proposals in 1979 and 1981, which were reiterated in their 2002 peace proposal, adopted by the entire Arab League.

Not a Defensive War

Yet Israel rejected all these peace proposals, and more, even though Israel's security was guaranteed in each one of them. Why? The historical record is clear that Israel's desire for additional land has been the single most important factor behind its expansionist policies. As David Ben-Gurion[4] said in 1938, "I favor partition of the country because when we become a strong power after the establishment of the state, we

3. Manachem Begin was Israel's prime minister from 1977 to 1983.   4. David Ben-Gurion was a Zionist leader who became Israel's first prime minister in 1948.

will abolish partition and spread throughout all of Palestine."

In sum, the 1967 war was not a purely defensive war on Israel's part, as Begin told us. The Israeli army met very little Palestinian resistance during the early years of the occupation. In the '60s and '70s, most Palestinian violence came from groups outside of the Occupied Territories. It is the Israeli desire to retain control over the West Bank, its expanding settlements and land appropriations that have sown the seeds of the situation we have today.

Israeli Actions

d) The Israeli occupation as the root cause of the violence. The main hallmark of the Israeli occupation has been the forcible expropriation of over half of the West Bank and Gaza for Jewish-only settlements, Jewish-only by-pass roads and Israeli closed military areas. These expropriations are possible only because of overwhelming Israeli military might and are, in and of themselves, acts of violence—just as armed robbery is an act of violence, even if no one is hurt. Can we really expect that no violent reaction to it would have occurred?

Israel's former Attorney General, Michael Ben-Yair stated point-blank in [the Israel newspaper] *Ha'aretz* (3/3/02) that, "We enthusiastically chose to become a colonial society, ignoring international treaties, expropriating lands, transferring settlers from Israel to the occupied territories, engaging in theft and finding justification for all these activities . . . In effect, we established an apartheid regime in the occupied territories immediately following their capture. That oppressive regime exists to this day."

e) How did the current level of violence come about? Palestinian attacks on Israeli civilians are well documented in our own media. And, while major Israeli incursions have gotten a good deal of attention, day-to-day excesses of the Israeli military have not been so widely reported. To get an accurate picture of the chain of events, let's look at the reports issued by human rights groups near the beginning of the current intifada.

Human Rights Violations

Human Rights Watch, for example, stated that, "Israeli security forces have committed by far the most serious and systematic violations. We documented excessive and indiscriminate use of lethal force, arbitrary killings, and collective punishment, including willful destruction of property and severe restrictions on movement that far exceed any possible military necessity."

B'Tselem is Israel's leading human rights group and their detailed analyses of the current intifada can be found at www.btselem.org. They concluded early on that, "In spite of claims to the contrary, Israel has not adopted a policy of restraint in its response to events in the Occupied Territories . . . Israel uses excessive and disproportionate force in dispersing demonstrations of unarmed Palestinians . . . Collective punishment, in the form of Israel's severe restrictions on Palestinians' movement in the Occupied Territories, makes life unbearable for hundreds of thousands with no justification." Collective punishment is illegal under international law.

The United Nations Commission on Human Rights reported the following, "There is considerable evidence of indiscriminate firing at civilians in the proximity of demonstrations and elsewhere (by Israeli troops) . . . The live ammunition employed includes high-velocity bullets which splinter on impact and cause the maximum harm. Equally disturbing is the evidence that many of the deaths and injuries inflicted were the result of head wounds and wounds to the upper body, which suggests an intention to cause serious bodily injury rather than restrain demonstrations . . . The measures of closure, curfew or destruction of property constitute violations of the Fourth Geneva Convention and human rights obligations binding upon Israel.". . .

The overwhelming consensus of these reports means that Israeli demands for the Palestinians to "stop the violence" turns reality on its head. The Palestinians have suffered almost four times the fatalities that Israel has in the current fighting, as well as tens of thousands of serious injuries. Furthermore, answering stone throwing with M-16 military weapons designed for battlefield use, or ineffective Molotov cocktails with very effective armored tanks and attack helicopters is simply not morally justifiable.

It is also important to keep in mind that many of Israel's current actions have been going on, in various degrees, for the last 35 years—systematic torture of Palestinians in Israeli jails, the forcible and illegal appropriation of over half the West Bank and Gaza by Israel for Jewish-only uses, daily humiliations and abuse at Israeli military checkpoints all over Palestinian land—these have combined to bring Palestinian anger to a boiling point.

Obstacles to Peace

In sum, we have seen that Israeli actions have served to seriously escalate the violence, and that Israel's stubborn refusal to end its occupation of the West Bank and Gaza Strip, even to the extent of just stopping its settlement activity, has been a major obstacle to any progress towards peace.

To be sure, Palestinian attacks on Israeli civilians have also been major obstacles towards such progress. Occupation and repression can never justify terrorism against civilians, but neither do terrorist acts by a few negate the Palestinian people's right to self-determination.

The best way to address these crimes is to end the occupation which inspires the Palestinians to commit them. Recent history has demonstrated clearly that support for such crimes, and the number of Palestinians willing to commit them, drops precipitously when the Palestinians have had hope for independence, and risen sharply in response to the intensifying occupation and expansion of settlements. . . .

End the Occupation

Any country has the right and the responsibility to protect its citizens, and Israel is no exception. But its policies for the last 35 years, and especially during the current intifada, have been based on the old adage, "the best defense is a good offense". While that's OK in football, in Israel that has translated into systematic torture or ill-treatment of literally hundreds of thousands of Palestinians in Israeli prisons, according to *B'Tselem* and other reputable groups. It means wanton cruelty being inflicted every day at military checkpoints, wanton destruction of Palestinian homes, and illegal strangling of Palestinian economic life, leading to extreme deprivation. And there is no other phrase than "war crimes" to accurately describe many of the actions of the IDF [Israeli

Defense Forces] during the attacks against the Palestinian civilian population in the spring of 2002. In short, the Israeli occupation of Palestinian territory is simply wrong—brutal, illegal and unnecessary.

We do agree that both sides have done poorly in advancing the cause of peace. As Jews, however, it is incumbent upon us to put our own house in order, above all else. As Americans, our responsibility is doubled. Our government has, through unprecedented financial and political support, allowed Israel to maintain its occupation and commit human rights violations with complete impunity. Thus, we are both responsible for the escalation and in a unique position to do something about it.

In the long-run, the only hope for a normal, peaceful life for the people of Israel is for their government to end their occupation of Palestinian land, allow the creation of a viable Palestinian state, and live and let live. The only other alternative is the current situation of endless bloodshed, which our silence, among other things, makes possible.

"*It is not the 1967 occupation that led to the Palestinians' rejection of peaceful coexistence and their pursuit of violence.*"

Israeli Occupation of Palestinian Lands Is Not a Source of Conflict

Efraim Karsh

Efraim Karsh is professor and director of Mediterranean studies at King's College, University of London. His books include *The Arab-Israeli Conflict: The Palestine War 1948*. In the following viewpoint, he rejects the view that Israel's occupation of the territories it acquired in the 1967 Six-Day War has been brutal or oppressive, or that it is the cause of violence between Palestinians and Israelis. Palestinian terrorism predates 1967, he argues, and has intensified even after Israel took steps in the 1990s to withdraw from the territories and permit Palestinian self-rule. It is Arab and Palestinian opposition to the existence of Israel itself that is a root cause of regional conflict, Karsh concludes.

As you read, consider the following questions:
1. What different meanings does the term "occupation" have regarding Israel, according to Karsh?
2. How have the living standards and conditions of Palestinians improved under Israeli rule, according to the author?
3. Why does Karsh attribute an increase in Palestinian terrorist attacks in the 1990s to an "*absence* of occupation"?

Efraim Karsh, "What Occupation?" *Commentary*, vol. 114, July/August 2002, pp. 46–51. Copyright © 2002 by the American Jewish Committee. Reproduced by permission of the publisher and the author.

No term has dominated the discourse of the Palestinian-Israeli conflict more than "occupation." For decades now, hardly a day has passed without some mention in the international media of Israel's supposedly illegitimate presence on Palestinian lands. This presence is invoked to explain the origins and persistence of the conflict between the parties, to show Israel's allegedly brutal and repressive nature, and to justify the worst anti-Israel terrorist atrocities. The occupation, in short, has become a catchphrase, and like many catchphrases it means different things to different people.

Different Conceptions of Occupation

For most Western observers, the term "occupation" describes Israel's control of the Gaza Strip and the West Bank, areas that it conquered during the Six-Day war of June 1967. But for many Palestinians and Arabs, the Israeli presence in these territories represents only the latest chapter in an uninterrupted story of "occupations" dating back to the very creation of Israel on "stolen" land. If you go looking for a book about Israel in the foremost Arab bookstore on London's Charing Cross Road, you will find it in the section labeled "Occupied Palestine." That this is the prevailing view not only among Arab residents of the West Bank and Gaza but among Palestinians living within Israel itself as well as elsewhere around the world is shown by the routine insistence on a Palestinian "right of return" that is meant to reverse the effects of the "1948 occupation"—i.e., the establishment of the state of Israel itself. . . .

Hanan Ashrawi, the most articulate exponent of the Palestinian cause, has been . . . forthright in erasing the line between post-1967 and pre-1967 "occupations." "I come to you today with a heavy heart," she told the now-infamous World Conference Against Racism in Durban last summer (2002), "leaving behind a nation in captivity held hostage to an ongoing *naqba* [catastrophe]":

> In 1948, we became subject to a grave historical injustice manifested in a dual victimization: on the one hand, the injustice of dispossession, dispersion, and exile forcibly enacted on the population. . . . On the other hand, those who remained were subjected to the systematic oppression and bru-

tality of an inhuman occupation that robbed them of all their rights and liberties.

This original "occupation"—that is again, the creation and existence of the state of Israel—was later extended, in Ashrawi's narrative, as a result of the Six-Day war:

Those of us who came under Israeli occupation in 1967 have languished in the West Bank, Jerusalem, and the Gaza Strip under a unique combination of military occupation, settler colonization, and systematic oppression. Rarely has the human mind devised such varied, diverse, and comprehensive means of wholesale brutalization and persecution.

Taken together, the charges against Israel's various "occupations" represent—and are plainly intended to be—a damning indictment of the entire Zionist enterprise. In almost every particular, they are also grossly false.

The Creation of Israel

In 1948, no Palestinian state was invaded or destroyed to make way for the establishment of Israel. From biblical times, when this territory was the state of the Jews, to its occupation by the British army at the end of World War I, Palestine had never existed as a distinct political entity but was rather part of one empire after another, from the Romans, to the Arabs, to the Ottomans. When the British arrived in 1917, the immediate loyalties of the area's inhabitants were parochial—to clan, tribe, village, town, or religious sect—and coexisted with their fealty to the Ottoman sultan-caliph as the religious and temporal head of the world Muslim community.

Under a League of Nations mandate explicitly meant to pave the way for the creation of a Jewish national home, the British established the notion of an independent Palestine for the first time and delineated its boundaries. In 1947, confronted with a determined Jewish struggle for independence, Britain returned the mandate to the League's successor, the United Nations, which in turn decided on November 29, 1947, to partition mandatory Palestine into two states: one Jewish, the other Arab.

The state of Israel was thus created by an internationally recognized act of national self-determination—an act, moreover, undertaken by an ancient people in its own homeland.

In accordance with common democratic practice, the Arab population in the new state's midst was immediately recognized as a legitimate ethnic and religious minority. As for the prospective Arab state, its designated territory was slated to include, among other areas, the two regions under contest today—namely, Gaza and the West Bank (with the exception of Jerusalem, which was to be placed under international control).

As is well known, the implementation of the UN's partition plan was aborted by the effort of the Palestinians and of the surrounding Arab states to destroy the Jewish state at birth. What is less well known is that even if the Jews had lost the war, their territory would not have been handed over to the Palestinians. Rather, it would have been divided among the invading Arab forces, for the simple reason that none of the region's Arab regimes viewed the Palestinians as a distinct nation. As the eminent Arab-American historian Philip Hitti described the common Arab view to an Anglo-American commission of inquiry in 1946, "There is no such thing as Palestine in history, absolutely not.". . .

No Conception of Palestinian Nationhood

Neither Egypt nor Jordan ever allowed Palestinian self-determination in Gaza and the West Bank—which were, respectively, the parts of Palestine conquered by them during the 1948–49 war. Indeed, even UN Security Council Resolution 242, which after the Six-Day war of 1967 established the principle of "land for peace" as the cornerstone of future Arab-Israeli peace negotiations, did not envisage the creation of a Palestinian state. . . .

At this time—we are speaking of the late 1960's—Palestinian nationhood was rejected by the entire international community, including the Western democracies, the Soviet Union (the foremost supporter of radical Arabism), and the Arab world itself. "Moderate" Arab rulers like the Hashemites in Jordan viewed an independent Palestinian state as a mortal threat to their own kingdom, while the Saudis saw it as a potential source of extremism and instability. Pan-Arab nationalists were no less adamantly opposed, having their own purposes in mind for the region. As late as 1974, Syrian President

Hafez al-Assad openly referred to Palestine as "not only a part of the Arab homeland but a basic part of southern Syria"; there is no reason to think he had changed his mind by the time of his death in 2000.

Nor, for that matter, did the populace of the West Bank and Gaza regard itself as a distinct nation. The collapse and dispersion of Palestinian society following the 1948 defeat had shattered an always fragile communal fabric, and the subsequent physical separation of the various parts of the Palestinian diaspora prevented the crystallization of a national identity. Host Arab regimes actively colluded in discouraging any such sense from arising. . . .

The Period After 1967

What, then, of the period after 1967, when these territories passed into the hands of Israel? Is it the case that Palestinians in the West Bank and Gaza have been the victims of the most "varied, diverse, and comprehensive means of wholesale brutalization and persecution" ever devised by the human mind?

At the very least, such a characterization would require a rather drastic downgrading of certain other well-documented 20th-century phenomena, from the slaughter of Armenians during World War I and onward through a grisly chronicle of tens upon tens of millions murdered, driven out, crushed under the heels of despots. By stark contrast, during the three decades of Israel's control, far fewer Palestinians were killed at Jewish hands than by King Hussein of Jordan in the single month of September 1970 when, fighting off an attempt by Yasir Arafat's PLO [Palestine Liberation Organization] to destroy his monarchy, he dispatched (according to the Palestinian scholar Yezid Sayigh) between 3,000 and 5,000 Palestinians, among them anywhere from 1,500 to 3,500 civilians. . . .

Such crude comparisons aside, to present the Israeli occupation of the West Bank and Gaza as "systematic oppression" is itself the inverse of the truth. It should be recalled, first of all, that this occupation did not come about as a consequence of some grand expansionist design, but rather was incidental to Israel's success against a pan-Arab attempt to destroy it.

Upon the outbreak of Israeli-Egyptian hostilities on June 5, 1967, the Israeli government secretly pleaded with King Hussein of Jordan, the de-facto ruler of the West Bank, to forgo any military action; the plea was rebuffed by the Jordanian monarch, who was loathe to lose the anticipated spoils of what was to be the Arabs' "final round" with Israel.

Thus it happened that, at the end of the conflict, Israel unexpectedly found itself in control of some one million Palestinians, with no definite idea about their future status and lacking any concrete policy for their administration. In the wake of the war, the only objective adopted by then-Minister of Defense Moshe Dayan was to preserve normalcy in the territories through a mixture of economic inducements and a minimum of Israeli intervention. The idea was that the local populace would be given the freedom to administer itself as it wished, and would be able to maintain regular contact with the Arab world via the Jordan River bridges. In sharp contrast with, for example, the U.S. occupation of postwar Japan, which saw a general censorship of all Japanese media and a comprehensive revision of school curricula, Israel made no attempt to reshape Palestinian culture. It limited its oversight of the Arabic press in the territories to military and security matters, and allowed the continued use in local schools of Jordanian textbooks filled with vile anti-Semitic and anti-Israel propaganda.

Economic and Social Progress

Israel's restraint in this sphere—which turned out to be desperately misguided—is only part of the story. The larger part, still untold in all its detail, is of the astounding social and economic progress made by the Palestinian Arabs under Israeli "oppression." At the inception of the occupation, conditions in the territories were quite dire. Life expectancy was low; malnutrition, infectious diseases, and child mortality were rife; and the level of education was very poor. Prior to the 1967 war, fewer than 60 percent of all male adults had been employed, with unemployment among refugees running as high as 83 percent. Within a brief period after the war, Israeli occupation had led to dramatic improvements in general well-being, placing the population of the territories ahead of most of their Arab neighbors.

In the economic sphere, most of this progress was the result of access to the far larger and more advanced Israeli economy: the number of Palestinians working in Israel rose from zero in 1967 to 66,000 in 1975 and 109,000 by 1986, accounting for 35 percent of the employed population of the West Bank and 45 percent in Gaza. Close to 2,000 industrial plants, employing almost half of the work force, were established in the territories under Israeli rule.

Asay. © 1996 by Creators Syndicate, Inc. Reprinted with permission.

During the 1970's, the West Bank and Gaza constituted the fourth fastest-growing economy *in the world*—ahead of such "wonders" as Singapore, Hong Kong, and Korea, and substantially ahead of Israel itself. . . .

Under Israeli rule, the Palestinians also made vast progress in social welfare. Perhaps most significantly, mortality rates in the West Bank and Gaza fell by more than two-thirds between 1970 and 1990, while life expectancy rose from 48 years in 1967 to 72 in 2000 (compared with an average of 68 years for all the countries of the Middle East and North Africa). Israeli medical programs reduced the infant-mortality rate of 60 per 1,000 live births in 1968 to 15 per 1,000 in 2000 (in Iraq the rate is 64, in Egypt 40, in Jordan 23, in Syria 22). And under a systematic program of inoculation, childhood diseases like polio, whooping cough, tetanus, and measles were eradicated.

No less remarkable were advances in the Palestinians' standard of living. By 1986, 92.8 percent of the population in the West Bank and Gaza had electricity around the clock, as compared to 20.5 percent in 1967; 85 percent had running water in dwellings, as compared to 16 percent in 1967; 83.5 percent had electric or gas ranges for cooking, as compared to 4 percent in 1967; and so on for refrigerators, televisions, and cars.

Finally, and perhaps most strikingly, during the two decades preceding the *intifada* of the late 1980's, the number of schoolchildren in the territories grew by 102 percent, and the number of classes by 99 percent, though the population itself had grown by only 28 percent. Even more dramatic was the progress in higher education. At the time of the Israeli occupation of Gaza and the West Bank, not a single university existed in these territories. By the early 1990's, there were seven such institutions, boasting some 16,500 students. Illiteracy rates dropped to 14 percent of adults over age 15, compared with 69 percent in Morocco, 61 percent in Egypt, 45 percent in Tunisia, and 44 percent in Syria.

Rise of the PLO

All this, as I have noted, took place against the backdrop of Israel's hands-off policy in the political and administrative spheres. Indeed, even as the PLO (until 1982 headquartered in Lebanon and thereafter in Tunisia) proclaimed its ongoing commitment to the destruction of the Jewish state, the Israelis did surprisingly little to limit its political influence in the territories. The publication of pro-PLO editorials was permitted in the local press, and anti-Israel activities by PLO supporters were tolerated so long as they did not involve overt incitement to violence. . . . As a result, the PLO gradually established itself as the predominant force in the territories, relegating the pragmatic traditional leadership to the fringes of the political system. . . .

But these things were not to be. By the mid-1970's, the PLO had made itself into the "sole representative of the Palestinian people," and in short order Jordan and Egypt washed their hands of the West Bank and Gaza. Whatever the desires of the people living in the territories, the PLO had vowed from the moment of its founding in the mid-1960's—well *before* the Six-Day war—to pursue its "revolution until victory," that is, until the destruction of the Jewish state. Once its position was secure, it proceeded to do precisely that.

By the mid-1990's, thanks to [the 1993] Oslo [accords], the PLO had achieved a firm foothold in the West Bank and Gaza. Its announced purpose was to lay the groundwork for Palestinian statehood but its real purpose was to do what it knew best—namely, create an extensive terrorist infrastructure and use it against its Israeli "peace partner." At first it did this tacitly, giving a green light to other terrorist organizations like Hamas and Islamic Jihad; then it operated openly and directly.

Israel's Withdrawal

But what did all this have to do with Israel's "occupation"? The declaration signed on the White House lawn in 1993 by the PLO and the Israeli government provided for Palestinian self-rule in the entire West Bank and the Gaza Strip for a transitional period not to exceed five years, during which Israel and the Palestinians would negotiate a permanent peace settlement. During this interim period the territories would be administered by a Palestinian Council, to be freely and democratically elected after the withdrawal of Israeli military forces both from the Gaza Strip and from the populated areas of the West Bank.

By May 1994, Israel had completed its withdrawal from the Gaza Strip (apart from a small stretch of territory containing Israeli settlements) and the Jericho area of the West Bank. On July 1, [PLO chairman] Yasir Arafat made his triumphant entry into Gaza. On September 28, 1995, despite Arafat's abysmal failure to clamp down on terrorist activities in the territories now under his control, the two parties signed an interim agreement, and by the end of the year Israeli forces had been withdrawn from the West Bank's populated areas with the exception of Hebron (where redeployment was completed in early 1997). On January 20, 1996, elections to the Palestinian Council were held, and shortly afterward both the Israeli civil administration and military government were dissolved.

The geographical scope of these Israeli withdrawals was relatively limited; the surrendered land amounted to some 30 percent of the West Bank's overall territory. But its impact on the Palestinian population was nothing short of revolutionary. At one fell swoop, Israel relinquished control over virtually all of the West Bank's 1.4 million residents. Since that time, nearly 60 percent of them—in the Jericho area and in the seven main cities of Jenin, Nablus, Tulkarm, Qalqilya, Ramallah, Bethlehem, and Hebron—have lived entirely under Palestinian jurisdiction. Another 40 percent live in towns, villages, refugee camps, and hamlets where the Palestinian Authority exercises civil authority but, in line with the Oslo accords, Israel has maintained "overriding responsibility for security." Some two percent of the West Bank's population—tens of thousands of Palestinians—continue to live in areas where Israel has complete control, but even there the Palestinian Authority maintains "functional jurisdiction."

In short, since the beginning of 1996, and certainly following the completion of the redeployment from Hebron in January 1997, 99 percent of the Palestinian population of the West Bank and the Gaza Strip have not lived under Israeli occupation. By no conceivable stretching of words can the anti-Israel violence emanating from the territories during these years be made to qualify as resistance to foreign occupation. In these years there has *been* no such occupation.

Terrorism and the Peace Process

If the stubborn persistence of Palestinian terrorism is not attributable to the continuing occupation, many of the worst outrages against Israeli civilians likewise occurred—contrary to the mantra of Palestinian spokesmen and their apologists—not at moments of breakdown in the Oslo "peace process" but at its high points, when the prospect of Israeli withdrawal appeared brightest and most imminent.

Suicide bombings, for example, were introduced in the atmosphere of euphoria only a few months after the historic Rabin-Arafat handshake on the White House lawn[1]: eight people were murdered in April 1994 while riding a bus in the town of Afula. Six months later, 21 Israelis were murdered on a bus in Tel Aviv. In the following year, five bombings took the lives of a further 38 Israelis. During the short-lived government of the dovish Shimon Peres (November 1995–May 1996), after the assassination of Yitzhak Rabin, 58 Israelis were murdered within the span of one week in three suicide bombings in Jerusalem and Tel Aviv.

Further disproving the standard view is the fact that terrorism was largely *curtailed* following Benjamin Netanyahu's election [as Israel's prime minister] in May 1996 and the consequent slowdown in the Oslo process. During Netanyahu's three years in power, some 50 Israelis were murdered in terrorist attacks—a third of the casualty rate during the Rabin government and a sixth of the casualty rate during Peres's term.

There was a material side to this downturn in terrorism as well. Between 1994 and 1996, the Rabin and Peres governments had imposed repeated closures on the territories in order to stem the tidal wave of terrorism in the wake of the Oslo accords. This had led to a steep drop in the Palestinian economy. With workers unable to get into Israel, unemployment rose sharply, reaching as high as 50 percent in Gaza. The movement of goods between Israel and the territories, as well as between the West Bank and Gaza, was seriously disrupted, slowing exports and discouraging potential private investment.

The economic situation in the territories began to improve during the term of the Netanyahu government, as the steep fall in terrorist attacks led to a corresponding decrease in closures. Real GNP per capita grew by 3.5 percent in 1997, 7.7 percent in 1998, and 3.5 percent in 1999, while unemployment was more than halved. By the beginning of 1999, ac-

---

1. Israeli Prime Minister Yitzhak Rabin and Palestinian leader Yasir Arafat made the historic handshake at the signing ceremony for the Oslo Accords on September 13, 1993.

cording to the World Bank, the West Bank and Gaza had fully recovered from the economic decline of the previous years.

Then, in still another turnabout, came Ehud Barak, who in the course of a dizzying six months in late 2000 and early 2001 offered Yasir Arafat a complete end to the Israeli presence, ceding virtually the entire West Bank and the Gaza Strip to the nascent Palestinian state together with some Israeli territory, and making breathtaking concessions over Israel's capital city of Jerusalem. To this, however, Arafat's response was war. Since its launch, the Palestinian campaign has inflicted thousands of brutal attacks on Israeli civilians—suicide bombings, drive-by shootings, stabbings, lynching, stonings—murdering more than 500 and wounding some 4,000.

In the entire two decades of Israeli occupation preceding the Oslo accords, some 400 Israelis were murdered; since the conclusion of that "peace" agreement, twice as many have lost their lives in terrorist attacks. If the occupation was the cause of terrorism, why was terrorism sparse during the years of actual occupation, why did it increase dramatically with the prospect of the end of the occupation, and why did it escalate into open war upon Israel's most far-reaching concessions ever? To the contrary, one might argue with far greater plausibility that the *absence* of occupation—that is, the withdrawal of close Israeli surveillance—is precisely what facilitated the launching of the terrorist war in the first place.

Palestinian Leadership Does Not Want Peace

There are limits to Israel's ability to transform a virulent enemy into a peace partner, and those limits have long since been reached. To borrow from Baruch Spinoza, peace is not the absence of war but rather a state of mind: a disposition to benevolence, confidence, and justice. From the birth of the Zionist movement until today, that disposition has remained conspicuously absent from the mind of the Palestinian leadership.

It is not the 1967 occupation that led to the Palestinians' rejection of peaceful coexistence and their pursuit of violence. Palestinian terrorism started well before 1967, and continued—and intensified—after the occupation ended in all but name. Rather, what is at fault is the perduring Arab view that the creation of the Jewish state was itself an original act of "inhuman occupation" with which compromise of any final kind is beyond the realm of the possible. Until that disposition changes, which is to say until a different leadership arises, the idea of peace in the context of the Arab Middle East will continue to mean little more than the continuation of war by other means.

"The Western nations have committed a litany of crimes against the Muslim world according to the Islamic opposition."

Foreign Intervention Is the Primary Cause of Conflict in the Middle East

William O. Beeman

The following viewpoint was written shortly after the September 11, 2001, terrorist attacks in which nineteen people from Saudi Arabia and other Middle Eastern nations hijacked jetliners and crashed them into the World Trade Center towers in New York and the Pentagon in Washington, D.C. In the following viewpoint, William O. Beeman argues that this act of terrorism has causes stemming from decades of meddling by Western nations, including the United States, in the Middle East. These actions, he argues, have led to divisiveness between Middle Eastern regimes and their people, initiated wars between Middle Eastern nations, and created in the region widespread antipathy toward the West. Beeman is an anthropology professor and specialist in Middle Eastern culture at Brown University in Rhode Island.

As you read, consider the following questions:

1. Who was the original leader of Islamic opposition to the West, according to Beeman?
2. How was the Middle East affected by the Cold War between the United States and the Soviet Union, in the author's view?
3. What role did the United States play in the creation of Saddam Hussein and the Taliban, according to Beeman?

William O. Beeman, "Why a Military Response Won't Work—Historic Roots of Middle East Grievances," *Pacific News Service*, September 19, 2001. Copyright © 2001 by *Pacific News Service*. Reproduced by permission.

The Bush administration's projected war on terrorism is designed to eradicate and delegitimize terrorists. Both aims are futile. The grievances of the terrorists who committed the horrendous attacks on New York and Washington on September 11 [2001] have deep and persistent roots going back more than 150 years. The terrorists harbor a hatred that will not die, and their grievances cannot be delegitimized through military attacks.

Middle Eastern opposition to the West is far from being a phenomenon invented by Osama bin Laden,[1] or the Taliban,[2] or for that matter Iran, Iraq or the Palestinians. It has grown consistently since the beginning of the 19th Century as an effective oppositional force both to the West and to local secular rulers. Western powers were blind to Middle Eastern opposition forces throughout the 20th Century because they were preoccupied with their own great power rivalry during this period.

The original leader of the opposition to the West was Jalal al-Din al-Afghani (1838–1897). Called the "Father of Islamic Modernism," Al-Afghani was educated in Iran, Afghanistan and India. He traveled throughout the Islamic world promulgating an "Islamic reform movement." Using an Islamic ideology helped him to transcend ethnic differences in the region, and preach a message all would understand. He sought to mobilize Muslim nations to fight against Western imperialism and gain military power through modern technology. Al-Afghani claimed that Britain, France and Russia in particular were operating in collusion with Middle Eastern rulers to rob the people of their patrimony through sweetheart deals for exploitation of natural and commercial resources in the region.

As a direct result of the efforts of Al-Afghani and his followers, groups such as the Muslim Brotherhood evolved throughout the region. These groups generally espoused three methods in their political and religious activity: personal piety coupled with evangelism, modernization without sacrificing core Islamic beliefs, and political resistance to secular regimes.

1. Osama bin Laden is the terrorist leader believed responsible for the September 11, 2001, terrorist attacks.   2. The Taliban is an Islamic regime in Afghanistan that harbored Osama bin Laden's terrorist network.

Crimes of Western Nations

The Western nations have committed a litany of crimes against the Muslim world according to the Islamic opposition. After World War I, the Middle Eastern peoples were treated largely as war prizes to be divided and manipulated for the good of the militarily powerful Europeans. The British and the French without consent or consultation on the part of the residents created every nation between the Mediterranean Sea and the Persian Gulf for their own benefit. This increased the resentment of the fundamentalists against the West and against the rulers installed by Westerners.

Remapping the Middle East

During the past two centuries, Western empires have mapped and re-mapped the Middle East repeatedly. They appointed, promoted, demoted, and dethroned local leaders to suit their strategic interests. One thing remained consistent and was omnipresent in their successive attempts to readjust borders and consolidate hegemonies: the availability of local demons to justify the frequent strategic reshaping and remapping.

One hundred and seventy years ago, Mohamed Ali of Egypt was declared a threat to free trade and was overthrown in favor of weak successors. Four decades later, Ahmed Urabi was removed from office and Egypt became a British occupied country (1882). A long line of successors, who pursued an independent course, provided the empire the necessary pretext to intervene. . . . A sense of threat kept the West busy fine tuning the empire to insure the perpetual dependency of the natives. Irrespective of their level of rationality, the Arab demons were declared a threat either to their own people, to their neighbors, to regional stability, to America's standard of living or even to US national security.

Naseer Aruri, *Counterpunch*, October 28, 2002.

During the Cold War, the United States and the Soviet Union fought over the Middle East nations like children over toys. Governments such as those of Egypt, the Sudan, Iraq, and Syria were constantly pressed to choose between East and West. The choice was often prompted by "gifts" of military support to sitting rulers. With ready sources of money and guns in either Washington or Moscow, Middle Eastern rulers could easily oppress the religious fundamentalists who opposed them. This added to the anger of the religious reformers. At this point the oppositionists abandoned political action through conventional political processes and turned to extra-governmental methods—terrorism—to make their dissatisfaction felt.

The United States became the sole representative of the West after 1972, when Great Britain, poor and humbled, could no longer afford to maintain a full military force in the region. Anxious to protect oil supplies from the Soviet Union, Washington propped up the Shah of Iran and the Saudi Arabian government in the ill-fated "Twin Pillars" strategy. This ended with the Iranian revolution, leaving America with a messy patchwork of military and political detritus. When Iran went to war with Iraq, the U.S. supported [Iraqi leader] Saddam Hussein to prevent Iran from winning. Anxious about Soviet incursions into Afghanistan, it propped up the Taliban. These two forces—Saddam and the Taliban—are very much an American creation.

The Final Blow

The final blow came when America finally had to confront its former client, Iraq, in the Gulf War. Americans established a military base on Saudi Arabian soil—considered sacred by pious Muslims. Saudi officials had been resisting this move for years, knowing that it would be politically dangerous both for them and for the United States. This action was the basis for Osama bin Laden's opposition to the United States.

All of this meddling only confirms the century-old assertion that the West was out to rob the people of the Middle East of their prerogatives and patrimony. The current revolutionaries in the region, including bin Laden, have political pedigrees leading directly back to the original reformer, Al-Afghani. Willy-nilly, the United States keeps reinforcing these old stereotypes. It is essential that we find a way to break this pattern, or we will be mired in these troubled relations forever.

*"Water is returning as the likeliest cause of
conflict in the Middle East."*

Scarce Water Could Cause Conflict in the Middle East

Adel Darwish

Fighting over scarce natural resources is often a cause of war
and conflict between nations. In the following viewpoint
Adel Darwish maintains that future water shortages are
likely to create conflicts among the nations of the Middle
East. The aridity of the region—as well as the area's growing population and political instability—will cause strife unless various nations agree to work together on water projects, the author contends. Darwish, a journalist, is coauthor
of *Water Wars: Coming Conflict in the Middle East.*

As you read, consider the following questions:

1. According to Darwish, what percentage of renewable
   water supplies does the Middle East use annually?
2. According to the author, which world leaders have
   suggested that water will be a likely cause of war in the
   Middle East.
3. How has the High Dam on the Nile affected
   development in Egypt, according to Darwish?

Adel Darwish, "Arid Waters," *Our Planet,* vol. 17, 1995. Copyright © 1995 by the
United Nations Environment Programme. Reproduced by permission.

A lone figure dressed all in black materializes out of the mirage where the dry sky glare meets the desert. As he moves closer, his attitude becomes tense. His eyes blaze as he reaches the well where a man is drinking, and with a single stroke of his sword, he strikes off the stranger's head.

That opening scene from the film *Lawrence of Arabia*—based on a story told by Lawrence himself—provides a stark warning that water in the arid environment of the Middle East is a matter of life and death.

Since the first oil well—discovered during drilling for water—gushed in Bahrain in 1932, countries have argued over borders in the hope of getting access to new riches. Now that most borders have been set, oil fields mapped and reserves accurately estimated, history is coming full circle. Water is returning as the likeliest cause of conflict in the Middle East. Whoever controls water or its distribution can dominate the region.

Searching for Water

From Turkey, the southern bastion of the North Atlantic Treaty Organization (NATO), down to Oman on the Indian Ocean, from the snow-helmeted Atlas Mountains in Morocco, to the depths of the Jordan valley, governments are searching for more water.

The population of the region will rise by 34 million within 30 years, and will then need 470 billion cubic metres of water annually—132 billion more than the total available supplies based on current levels of consumption (even assuming that there will be a 2 per cent improvement in conservation each year.

Water is being used faster than nature can replace it. On average the region uses 155 per cent of its renewable water supplies each year. Individual countries' consumption ranges from the Libyan Arab Jamahiriya at 374 per cent to Bahrain at 102 per cent.

In 1994, the World Bank estimated that renewable per capita water supplies would fall fivefold in the space of one lifetime—1960–2025—to 667 cubic metres per year (well below the official level of water scarcity). In several countries this will barely cover basic human needs into the twenty-first century.

When President Anwar Sadat signed the peace treaty with Israel, he said that Egypt will never go to war again, except to protect its water resources. King Hussein of Jordan has said he will never again go to war with Israel, except over water. [Former] United Nations Secretary-General Boutros Boutros-Ghali has warned bluntly that water will cause the next war in the area.

In 1989 Israel withdrew hydrologists and surveyors who were investigating building a dam in Ethiopia on the Blue Nile, which provides 85 per cent of Egypt's water, amid threats of war in the People's Assembly in Cairo. In 1990 Turkey stopped the flow of the Euphrates altogether to fill its Ataturk Dam. The media of the two downstream nations, the Syrian Arab Republic and Iraq, united in denouncing the stoppage and there were threats of armed retaliation. The CIA gave its opinion in 1992 that trouble between Turkey and the Syrian Arab Republic over water was the likeliest prospect for a full-scale war in the region.

Few agreements have been reached about sharing such cross-border water resources as international aquifers or the rivers of the region. Two of the three main aquifers lie for the most part under the West Bank of the Jordan. Muslim fundamentalists have recently made it *Jihad*—a sacred mission—to recover water used by Israeli settlers, for the use of Muslims.

Limits to International Law

International law on shared water courses, rivers or cross-border aquifers is unclear. Governments and organizations negotiate agreements using a mixture of customary use and local and traditional laws, and the established right of use over an unspecified period of time. Such mixtures are often contradictory and in themselves a cause of conflict. There are few, if any, precedents that the United Nations International Law Commission or the International Court of Justice could cite to establish rules to arbitrate on water sharing.

Since the late 1940s, the World Bank has insisted that agreements are concluded between riparian nations on sharing the benefits of the water projects that it helps to finance. It also commissions independent studies to modify plans and alter designs to minimize the harm that the project might inflict on neighbouring peoples.

But when governments finance their own water schemes, there is no provision in international law to stop them imposing their will on neighbours, uprooting ethnic minorities or inflicting far reaching and lasting effects on the environment.

Israel, Palestinians and Water

[In the] bloody Israeli-Palestinian conflict, the region's competing actors are jockeying to maintain control of the available water. The combination of a naturally arid environment, years of drought, and poor planning is proving to be dry tinder in a combustible atmosphere.

Take Israel's far Right infrastructure minister Effie Eitam's order halting all Palestinian well drilling in the West Bank in October 2002, alleging that Palestenians were runing a 'water Intifada' against Israel through unauthorized tapping. Besides endangering the crippled Palestinian farming sector, the move threatened the tens of millions of dollars of foreign aid money spent on unfinished water infrastructure.

The next day Fatil Qawash, the head of Palestinian Water Authority, was irate. 'Year by year, we have less and less water. No more water in the springs, no more water from the weather and at the same time the Israeli side has applied a policy to reduce the water that they supply us, he said. 'Now they are blaming us for stealing water. This is not stealing water. This is our water.'

There lies the crux of the problem. Israel has access to both high-tech solutions and water from the occupied West Bank. Palestinians, on the other hand, have far less water to work with and remain caught in the terms of agreements signed with Israel years ago. Palestinian long-term planning remains tentative as long as the issue of their regional water rights is unresolved.

Charmaine Seitz, *New Internationalist*, 2003.

To taunt the late Egyptian leader Colonel Gamal Abdel Nasser in the 1950s, Britain unwisely induced the World Bank to turn down Egypt's request to finance the building of the High Dam on the Nile near Aswan. The Soviet Union was only too happy to finance and construct instead, winning a foothold in the region. The dam was built away from international supervision and Colonel Nasser turned down alternative projects, which would have been environmentally and economically more sound. 'Here are joined the political, national and military battles of the Egyptian people, welded together like the gigantic mass of rock that has blocked the course of the ancient Nile,' he told the crowds in May 1964 when the first phase of the project was complete.

The dam is providing multiple benefits to farmers and generating about twice the national requirement for electricity. But it has also had less benign effects. It has damaged valuable ecosystems and fishing grounds (the sardines that once bred in the Nile have almost disappeared from the Mediterranean), eroded beaches by changing the hydrology of the area (the coastal defences built on the Mediterranean coast in the 1940s have been overwhelmed since the dam was built) and deprived the Nile Valley and delta of the silt and natural fertilizers which had nourished its agriculture for thousands of years.

An Ultimate Solution

The ultimate solution to the water problems of the region is to shift production and economic patterns away from agriculture, the major user of water, and import food supplies instead—which would be cheaper than building unrealistic water projects—or to grow crops that consume less water for exports. But political insecurity and distrust of neighbours make this difficult for governments to do.

Similar problems dog plans for a joint Jordanian-Israeli Canal from the Red Sea to the Dead Sea, which would use the 100 metre drop between the seas to generate electricity for desalination: it can only work when all neighbours agree to cooperate on peaceful terms. Even if it happens, demand will soon outstrip supply if the nations in the region continue to abuse its water resources.

It remains likely that water conflict will add to the troubles of the region. 'A time may well come,' one leading politician of the area said privately, 'when we have to calculate whether a small swift war might be economically more rewarding than putting up with a drop in our water supplies'.

Periodical Bibliography

The following articles have been selected to supplement the diverse views presented in this chapter.

Fouad Ajami "The Endless Claim (Palestinian State)," *U.S. News & World Report*, January 8, 2001.

Mohammed Aldouri "Iraq States Its Case," *New York Times*, October 17, 2002.

Perry Anderson "Scurrying Towards Bethlehem (Zionism and the Israeli-Palestinian Conflict)," *New Left Review*, July/August 2001.

Arnaud De Borchgrave "Terrorism Is a Common Threat in Struggles for Independence," *Insight on the News*, May 6, 2002.

Larry Derfner et al. "Spiral of Violence," *U.S. News & World Report*, March 18, 2002.

James O.C. Jonah "The Middle East Conflict: The Palestinian Dimension," *Global Governance*, October–December 2002.

Avi Jorisch "The Middle East Explodes—The Recent Troubles," *World & I*, February 2002.

Joe Klein "How Israel Is Wrapped Up in Iraq," *Time*, February 10, 2003.

Dennis Kucinich "The Bloodstained Path," *The Progressive*, November 2002.

Johanna McGeary "Dissecting the Case: The Administration's Rationale for War with Iraq Is Based on New and Old Evidence—as Well as Passionate Conviction," *Time*, February 10, 2003.

New Statesman "Middle East: No Goodies or Baddies," March 18, 2002.

Fiamma Nirenstein "How Suicide Bombers Are Made," *Commentary*, September 2001.

John Pilger "If You Got Your News Only from the Television, You Would Have No Idea of the Roots of the Middle East Conflict, or That the Palestinians Are Victims of an Illegal Military Occupation," *New Statesman*, July 1, 2002.

Danny Rubenstein "Israel at Fifty," *Nation*, May 4, 1998.

Jonathan Schanzer "Palestinian Uprisings Compared," *Middle East Quarterly*, Summer 2002.

Somini Sengupta	"In Israel and Lebanon, Talk of War over Water," *New York Times*, October 16, 2002.
Joseph C. Wilson	"A 'Big Cat' with Nothing to Lose; Leaving Hussein No Hope Will Trigger His Worst Weapons," *Los Angeles Times*, February 6, 2003.
Mortimer B. Zuckerman	"Clear and Compelling Proof," *U.S. News & World Report*, February 10, 2003.

CHAPTER 2

How Does Islam Affect the Middle East?

Chapter Preface

In July 2002 the United Nations Development Programme (UNDP) published a report that examined the development of twenty-two Arab nations (as well as Palestinians in Israel) using measurements ranging from per capita income growth to Internet usage statistics. Written by Arab scholars, the *Arab Human Development Report 2002* concluded that while the region, blessed with natural resources, has made much progress in some areas, including poverty reduction, these nations lagged behind the rest of the world in their social, political, and economic development. One of the report's striking findings was that more than half of Arab youth polled expressed a desire to leave their country and move to Europe or North America. The report's authors identified three main areas in which modern Arab culture was lacking: political freedom, knowledge development, and the treatment and status of women.

The report did not directly discuss or implicate Islam as a cause of these social problems, yet many argue that the role of this religion in hampering development cannot be overlooked. Of the three major world religions that originated in the Middle East—Judaism, Christianity, and Islam—it is Islam, founded by the Arabian prophet Muhammad in the 600s, that became the dominant religion in the region. Presently more than 90 percent of the Middle East's people, including most Arabs, Iranians, and Turks, are Muslims (Christians of various sects make up about 7 percent of the region's population, while Jews, most of whom live in Israel, make up 1 percent). Islam is not only the religion of most of the people, but it is the official state religion of many Middle East nations. As a result, Islamic clerics play a major role in the politics of these countries. In Saudi Arabia, for example, other religions are forbidden, and Islamic law or *sharia*—based on the Koran, Islam's holy book—is the foundation of its legal system.

Whether and how Islam contributes to underdevelopment is a matter of debate. The fact that women in most Arab countries lack equal political and civil rights—one of the problems identified in the UNDP report—has served as a flash-point issue for those debating the role of Islam in Middle East development. Saudi Arabia serves as a good example. In Saudi Arabia, women face serious gender discrimination, including segregation in public areas, lack of freedom of movement (including the right to drive automobiles), less rights in criminal trials, and limited participation in government. Some observers argue that Islam is the primary cause of these gender inequities. Author Ibn Warraq asserts that "Islam is the fundamental cause of the repression of Muslim women. . . . Islam has always considered women as creatures inferior in every way: physically, intellectually, and morally." But others argue that gender discrimination is more a product of Arab culture and customs rather than Islamic teachings. "Many of the most repressive practices ascribed to Islam are based on cultural traditions . . . or contested interpretations," writes religion journalist Teresa Watanabe. "Even Saudi-trained scholars, for instance, agree that the kingdom's ban on women driving is not grounded in the Koran or the prophet's traditions."

Islam's role in determining the status of women in the Middle East is one of several issues discussed in the following chapter. Authors examine how Islam will shape future development of the region.

*"For the Middle East today, moderate Islam
may be democracy's last hope."*

Islam Can Be Compatible with Democracy

Ray Takeyh

Of all the nations in the Middle East, only Israel fully quali-
fies as a democracy in which its citizens have the right to elect
or vote out governments. Other Middle East countries are
ruled by hereditary monarchs, military rulers, or lifetime
presidents. Some people have speculated that longstanding
cultural traditions, including the Islamic religion, prevent the
region from becoming more democratic. In the following
viewpoint Ray Takeyh takes issue with the view that Middle
East Muslims are not capable of democracy. Many people in
the region have been inspired by the emergence of democracies in other parts of the world, he argues, and a new generation of Islamic thinkers is attempting to formulate ways of
replacing existing Middle East regimes with democratic governments that are consistent with Islamic values. Takeyh is a
research fellow at the Washington Institute for Near East
Policy; his works include *The Receding Shadow of the Prophet:
Radical Islamic Movements in the Modern Middle East.*

As you read, consider the following questions:

1. Why is the choice between "Islam" and "modernity" a
simplistic one, according to Takeyh?
2. Why does the author consider extremist militant Islam
to be on the decline?
3. How might future Islamic democracies differ from those
in Western nations, according to the author?

The televised footage of an airliner crashing into the World Trade Center [during the September 11, 2001, terrorist attacks on America] is now the prevailing image of Islam. Media pundits decry anti-Muslim bigotry and hasten to remind the public that Islam is a religion of peace and tolerance, notwithstanding the actions of an extremist minority. But in the same breath many of those pundits warn of a clash of civilizations—a war that pits the secular, modernized West against a region mired in ancient hatreds and fundamentalist rage.

A Third Option

This simplistic choice between "Islam" and "modernity" ignores a third option that is emerging throughout the Middle East. Lost amidst the din of cultural saber-rattling are the voices calling for an Islamic reformation: A new generation of theological thinkers, led by figures such as Iranian President Muhammad Khatami and Tunisian activist Rached Ghannouchi, is reconsidering the orthodoxies of Islamic politics. In the process, such leaders are demonstrating that the region may be capable of generating a genuinely democratic order, one based on indigenous values. For the Middle East today, moderate Islam may be democracy's last hope. For the West, it might represent one of the best long-term solutions to "winning" the war against Middle East terrorism.

Militant Islam continues to tempt those on the margins of society (and guides anachronistic forces such as Afghanistan's Taliban and Palestine's Islamic Jihad), but its moment has passed. In Iran, the Grand Ayatollah's autocratic order[1] degenerated into corruption and economic stagnation. Elsewhere, the Islamic radicals' campaign of terror—such as Gamma al-Islamiyya in Egypt and Hezbollah in Lebanon—failed to produce any political change, as their violence could not overcome the brutality of the states they encountered. The militants' incendiary rhetoric and terrorism only triggered public revulsion, not revolutions and mass uprisings. Indeed, the Arab populace may have returned to reli-

1. Ayatollah Khomeini led a revolution and established an Islam-based government in Iran in 1979.

gion over the last two decades, but they turned to a religion that was tolerant and progressive, not one that called for a violent displacement of the existing order with utopias.

Political Islam as a viable reform movement might have petered out were it not for one minor detail: The rest of the world was changing. The collapse of the Soviet Union and the emergence of democratic regimes in Eastern Europe, Latin America, and East Asia electrified the Arab populace. Their demands were simple but profound. As one Egyptian university student explained in 1993, "I want what they have in Poland, Czechoslovakia. Freedom of thought and freedom of speech." In lecture halls, street cafes, and mosques, long dormant ideas of representation, identity, authenticity, and pluralism began to arise.

A New Generation

The task of addressing the population's demand for a pluralistic society consistent with traditional values was left to a new generation of Islamist thinkers, who have sought to legitimize democratic concepts through the reinterpretation of Islamic texts and traditions. Tunisia's Ghannouchi captures this spirit of innovation by stressing, "Islam did not come with a specific program concerning life. It is our duty to formulate this program through interaction between Islamic precepts and modernity." Under these progressive readings, the well-delineated Islamic concept of *shura* (consultation) compels a ruler to consider popular opinion and establishes the foundation for an accountable government. In a modern context, such consultation can be implemented through the standard tools of democracy: elections, plebiscites, and referendums. The Islamic notion of *jima* (consensus) has been similarly accommodated to serve as a theological basis for majoritarian rule. For Muslim reformers, Prophet Mohammed's injunction that "differences of opinion within my community is a sign of God's mercy" denotes prophetic approbation of diversity of thought and freedom of speech.

The new generation of Islamists has quickly embraced the benefits wrought by modernization and globalization in order to forge links between Islamist groups and thinkers in the various states of the Middle East. Through mosques, Islamists easily distribute pamphlets, tracts, and cassettes of Islamic thinkers and writers. In today's [2001] Middle East, one can easily find the Egyptian Brotherhood's magazine *Al-Dawa* in bookstores in the Persian Gulf while the Jordanian Islamist daily *Al-Sabil* enjoys wide circulation throughout the Levant. The advent of the Internet has intensified such cross-pollination, as most Islamist journals, lectures, and conference proceedings are posted on the Web. The writings of Iranian philosopher Abdol Karim Soroush today appear in Islamic curricula across the region, and Egypt's Islamist liberal Hassan Hanafi commands an important audience in Iran's seminaries.

Islamic Democracy

In the future, such Islamists will likely vie to succeed the region's discredited military rulers and lifetime presidents. But what will a prospective Islamic democracy look like? Undoubtedly, Islamic democracy will differ in important ways from the model that evolved in post-Reformation Europe. Western systems elevated the primacy of the individual above the community and thus changed the role of religion from that of the public conveyor of community values to a private guide for individual conscience. In contrast, an Islamic democracy's attempt to balance its emphasis on reverence with the popular desire for self-expression will impose certain limits on individual choice. An Islamic polity will support fundamental tenets of democracy—namely, regular elections, separation of powers, an independent judiciary, and institutional opposition—but it is unlikely to be a libertarian paradise.

The question of gender rights is an excellent example of the strengths—and limits—of an Islamic democracy. The Islamists who rely on women's votes, grass-roots activism, and participation in labor markets cannot remain deaf to women's demands for equality. Increasingly, Islamic reformers suggest the cause of women's failure to achieve equality is not religion but custom. The idea of black-clad women passively accepting the dictates of superior males is the province of Western caricatures. Iran's parliament, cabinet, and universities are populated with women, as are the candidate lists for Islamic opposition parties in Egypt and

Cause for Optimism

There is . . . cause for cautious optimism. Recent polls show that Arabs and Muslims, while more culturally conservative and religious than most of the democratic world, share many of the same aspirations for freedom and democracy that we do. It's also a positive that the Arab countries tend to be ethnically homogenous: It's easier to make democracy work in societies that don't have violent ethnic animosities. A number of Arab countries possess significant wealth and have achieved relatively high levels of economic development, making it possible to avoid the instability that often arises from grinding poverty. Moreover, these societies possess the immense untapped potential of women, who have long been denied their proper place in political and economic life.

The West has a crucial role to play in these developments. For many years the U.S. and the rest of the democratic world were hesitant to apply to Arab countries the kind of pressure for democratic change that was so helpful in Central and Eastern Europe, Latin America, and parts of Asia. But this policy is beginning to change. . . .

Our strategy will become stronger if it emphasizes that there is nothing inherently Islamic or Arabic about dictatorship and tyranny—that, just like the citizens of Europe, today's Muslims have the prerequisites for entering the democratic community of nations.

Adriar Karatnycky, *National Review*, Decmber 31, 2002.

Turkey. But while an Islamic democracy will not impede women's integration into public affairs, it will impose restrictions on them, particularly in the realm of family law and dress codes. In such an order, women can make significant progress, yet in important ways they may still lag behind their Western counterparts. Moderate Islamists are likely to be most liberal in the realm of economic policy. The failure of command economies in the Middle East and the centrality of global markets to the region's economic rehabilitation have made minimal government intervention appealing to Islamist theoreticians. Moreover, a privatized economy is consistent with classical Islamic economic theory and its well-established protection of market and commerce. The Islamist parties have been among the most persistent critics of state restrictions on trade and measures that obstruct opportunities for middle-class entrepreneurs.

International Implications

The international implications of the emergence of Islamic democracies are also momentous. While revolutionary Islam could not easily coexist with the international system, moderate Islam can serve as a bridge between civilizations. The coming to power of moderate Islamists throughout the Middle East might lead to a lessening of tensions both within the region and between it and other parts of the world. Today, security experts talk of the need to "drain the swamps" and deprive terrorists of the state sponsorship that provides the protection and funding to carry out their war against the West. Within a more open and democratic system, dictatorial regimes would enjoy less freedom to support terrorism or engage in military buildups without any regard for economic consequences.

Ultimately, however, the integration of an Islamic democracy into global democratic society would depend on the willingness of the West to accept an Islamic variant on liberal democracy. Islamist moderates, while conceding that there are in fact certain "universal" democratic values, maintain that different civilizations must be able to express these values in a context that is acceptable and appropriate to their particular region. Moderate Islamists, therefore, will continue to struggle against any form of U.S. hegemony, whether in political or cultural terms, and are much more comfortable with a multipolar, multi-"civilizational" international system. Khatami's call for a "dialogue of civilizations" presupposes that there is no single universal standard judging the effectiveness of democracy and human rights.

Certainly, the West should resist totalitarian states who use the rhetoric of democracy while rejecting its essence through false claims of cultural authenticity. But even though an Islamic democracy will resist certain elements of post-Enlightenment liberalism, it will still be a system that features regular elections, accepts dissent and opposition parties, and condones a free press and division of power between branches of state. As such, any fair reading of Islamic democracy will reveal that it is a genuine effort to conceive a system of government responsive to popular will. And this effort is worthy of Western acclaim.

2

"Democratic values do not slumber in the subconsious of the Islamic world."

Islam May Not Be Compatible with Democracy

Milton Viorst

The following viewpoint was written shortly after U.S.-led military action ended the dictatorship of Iraqi leader Saddam Hussein in April 2003. Journalist and author Milton Viorst argues that if free elections were to be held in Iraq, Hussein's regime could well be replaced by an Islamic theocracy in which democratic freedoms as practiced in the West would be restricted. He argues that similar results would occur throughout the Middle East from attempts to democratize Middle Eastern nations. Viorst raises the question of whether Islam—the dominant religion in the region—is compatible with democracy. Viorst is a veteran Middle East journalist and the author of *In the Shadow of the Prophet: The Struggle for the Soul of Islam.*

As you read, consider the following questions:

1. What distinction does Viorst draw between countries in Europe and the Middle East?
2. What was so important about the Renaissance to the development of democracy, according to the author?
3. What conclusions does Viorst draw about the American government's vision of a transformed Middle East?

Iraq's Shiites,[1] 60% of the population, most of them fervently religious, have stunned U.S. officials who gave us the [2003] war to overthrow Saddam Hussein. Not only do they reject our occupation, but they also dismiss the Western-style democracy that we were assured they would welcome.

It took hardly more than recent [April 2003] full-color pictures in newspapers and on television of Shiite men flagellating themselves until blood streamed from their flesh to make the case that we are dealing with people we don't know. Ironically, Hussein's regime had barred self-flagellation as barbaric. For believers, his fall did not mean freedom to adopt a constitution and elect a parliament; it meant freedom to suffer the stings of whips for a martyr who died 13 centuries ago[2] and to demand an Islamic state.

When communism died at the end of the 1980s, Vaclav Havel, the poet who became president of Czechoslovakia, declared that "democratic values slumbered in the subconscious of our nations." His words suggest that these nations waited only for the sunshine of spring to awake to the democracy that had lain dormant within them. Indeed, societies liberated from communism, including Russia, navigated the currents of Western values to adopt democratic systems, though they sometimes perilously scraped the rocks. So did the European countries delivered from fascism after World War II—Italy and Germany, then Spain and Portugal.

But democratic values do not slumber in the subconscious of the Islamic world. Free elections threaten to bring religious extremists to power in Egypt, Jordan, Pakistan and even Turkey, which has been working at democracy for nearly a century. Were free elections held in Saudi Arabia, fanatics would surely triumph. In 1992, elections brought Algeria to the edge of Islamic rule, triggering a civil war that still rages. Given the substantial divisions in Iraq's population, and the power of religion within its Shiite majority, free elections there would probably produce the same outcome.

Years ago, I asked an elderly philosopher in Damascus,

---

1. Shiites are followers of the Shia branch of Islam. They have long been suppressed in Iraq by Saddam Hussein's Sunni-dominated regime.   2. Imam Hussein bin Ali, the grandson of the prophet Mohammed.

Syria, to explain the difficulty the Arabs have in mastering democracy, and he answered, ruefully: "The Islamic world never had a Renaissance." What he meant, I later understood, was that the steps toward secularism that Western society first took in mid-millennium are yet to be taken—or, at best, have been taken only hesitantly—within Islam.

The Renaissance's Importance

The seminal notion that the Renaissance introduced to the West was that mankind, not God, is at the hub of the social universe. It held reason as important as faith, and urged men and women to claim responsibility, free of clergy, for their own lives.

Under the influence of texts from ancient Greece, Muslims in their Golden Age considered and rejected these ideas before passing the texts on to Europe. After triggering the Renaissance, the ideas led, over quarrelsome centuries, to the Reformation, the Enlightenment and the Scientific Revolution. While Islam remained wedded to desert tradition, Europe created a civilization imbued with a sense of individual identity, in which men and women asserted rights apart from those of the community. These ideas, for better or worse, became the foundation of the secular culture that characterizes Western civilization today.

Religion by no means disappeared. Instead, it was redefined as a personal bond, a relationship of choice, between the individual and God. The redefinition made Westerners comfortable separating worship from the state. True, segments of the Catholic Church, Orthodox Jewry and evangelical Protestantism still question this arrangement. But the secular idea constitutes the foundation of mainstream Western values. Without it, democracy—and the civil society that, along with the press, supports it—would be impossible.

Islam and Everyday Life

This process has largely bypassed Islamic society. Muslims like to say that "Islam isn't just a religion; it's a way of life." What they mean is that there is no barrier between faith and the everyday world, between what is sacred and what is profane. It is not so much that Muslims are more pious than

Westerners. It is that the imperatives of the culture impose limits on diversity of outlook, whether religious or social. These imperatives suppress the demand for personal identity, leaving believers with little tolerance for the free and open debate necessarily at democracy's core.

Ironically, Hussein's Baath regime once promised to introduce Iraq to secularism. It went further than any other Arab state in emancipating women, curbing clerical power, promoting literature and arts and advancing universal literacy within a framework of modern education. Its tragedy is that these seeds of democracy were subsumed under the world's most brutal tyranny, crushing their human potential. After 1,400 years of Islamic conservatism and 25 of Hussein, there is little likelihood that a disposition to democracy slumbers in Iraq's psyche.

From President [George W.] Bush on down, officials who are presiding over the rebuilding of Iraq would be wise to remember that the values at our system's heart have been a thousand years in the making. No doubt Iraq's Shiite majority is happy at Hussein's downfall, but American lectures on the virtues of replacing him with democratic rule fall on uncomprehending ears. So much must first be done to lay a groundwork of individual freedom and responsibility, values that Iraqis must willingly embrace. At the moment, the majority is more comfortable with the familiar idea of Islamic government. Would that it were otherwise, but the administration's vision of a Middle East reshaped by Western democracy, starting with Iraq, is naive and, moreover, delusive.

"Resort to political violence . . . became the preferred option after Iran's revolution emboldened [Islamic] fundamentalists everywhere."

Islamic Fundamentalism Fosters Violence in the Middle East

Martin Kramer

Martin Kramer, a senior associate and former director of the Moshe Dayan Center for Middle Eastern and African Studies at Tel Aviv University in Israel, has written numerous articles and books on the Middle East and Islam. In the following viewpoint he argues that fundamentalist Islam has led to political violence in the Middle East. Islamic fundamentalists believe that the tenets of Islam should govern all facets of life, from private conduct to state and public affairs. Although they often claim that their beliefs do not justify violence, Kramer contends, fundamentalists have resorted to war, assassination, and terrorism in an attempt to spread the influence of Islam throughout the Middle East and the world.

As you read, consider the following questions:

1. According to Kramer, what evidence led an Arab critic to compare Sayyid al-Afghani's thinking to fascism?
2. What is the "double identity" of the Muslim Brethren, according to the author?
3. What doctrine of Ruhollah Khomeini's led to the success of an Islamic revolution in Iran, according to Kramer?

Martin Kramer, "The Drive for Power," *Middle East Quarterly*, June 1996.

As the twentieth century closes, two words, Islam and fundamentalism, have become intimately linked in English usage. *The Concise Oxford Dictionary of Current English* now defines *fundamentalism* as the "strict maintenance of ancient or fundamental doctrines of any religion, especially Islam." However problematic this formula, it does acknowledge that fundamentalism in Islam is today the most visible and influential of all fundamentalisms.

The nature of fundamentalist Islam, and even the use of the term, is hotly debated. But this debate is largely a self-indulgent exercise of analysts. Within Islam, there are Muslims who have created an "-ism" out of Islam—a coherent ideology, a broad strategy, and a set of political preferences. They do not defy definition. They defy the world.

The Contradictions of Fundamentalist Islam?

What is fundamentalist Islam? Its contradictions seem to abound. On the one hand, it manifests itself as a new religiosity, reaffirming faith in a transcendent God. On the other hand, it appears as a militant ideology, demanding political action now. Here it takes the form of a populist party, asking for ballots. There it surges forth as an armed phalanx, spraying bullets. One day its spokesmen call for a *jihad* (sacred war) against the West, evoking the deepest historic resentments. Another day, its leaders appeal for reconciliation with the West, emphasizing shared values. Its economic theorists reject capitalist materialism in the name of social justice, yet they rise to the defense of private property. Its moralists pour scorn on Western consumer culture as debilitating to Islam, yet its strategists avidly seek to buy the West's latest technologies in order to strengthen Islam.

Faced with these apparent contradictions, many analysts in the West have decided that fundamentalism defies all generalization. Instead they have tried to center discussion on its supposed "diversity." For this purpose, they seek to establish systems of classification by which to sort out fundamentalist movements and leaders. The basic classification appears in many different terminological guises, in gradations of subtlety.

We need to be careful of that emotive label, 'fundamentalism', and distinguish, as Muslims do, between revivalists, who choose to take the practice of their religion most devoutly, and fanatics or extremists, who use this devotion for political ends.

So spoke the Prince of Wales in a 1993 address, summarizing the conventional wisdom in a conventional way. The belief that these categories really exist, and that experts can sort fundamentalists neatly into them, is the sand on which weighty policies are now being built.

Radical Islamic Movements

Radical Islamic movements in general have clearly identified their enemy: the regimes in the Islamic worlds which practice non-Islamic law: the West which has been undermining Islam from within and corrupting it with its norms of permissiveness in order to totter it and replace it; and Israel-Zionism—the Jews, who are intrinsically the enemies of Allah and humanity, in addition to their being an arm of the West in the heart of the islamic world. The enemy must be depicted in evil terms so as to make it a free prey for Muslims to attack and destroy. Rhetorical delegitimation of their enemy is an essential step towards making the use of violence permissible, even desirable, against him. Hence the systematic and virulent onslaughts of those movements against what they perceive as their enemies, domestic and external.

Raphael Israeli, *Terrorism and Political Violence*, Autumn, 1997.

Fundamentalist Islam remains an enigma precisely because it has confounded all attempts to divide it into tidy categories. "Revivalist" becomes "extremist" (and vice versa) with such rapidity and frequency that the actual classification of any movement or leader has little predictive power. They will not stay put. This is because fundamentalist Muslims, for all their "diversity," orbit around one dense idea. From any outside vantage point, each orbit will have its apogee and perigee. The West thus sees movements and individuals swing within reach, only to swing out again and cycle right through every classification. Movements and individuals arise in varied social and political circumstances, and have their own distinctive orbits. But they will not defy the gravity of their idea.

The idea is simple: Islam must have power in this world. It is the true religion—the religion of God—and its truth is manifest in its power. When Muslims believed, they were powerful. Their power has been lost in modern times because Islam has been abandoned by many Muslims, who have reverted to the condition that preceded God's revelation to the Prophet Muhammad. But if Muslims now return to the original Islam, they can preserve and even restore their power.

That return, to be effective, must be comprehensive; Islam provides the one and only solution to all questions in this world, from public policy to private conduct. It is not merely a religion, in the Western sense of a system of belief in God. It possesses an immutable law, revealed by God, that deals with every aspect of life, and it is an ideology, a complete system of belief about the organization of the state and the world. This law and ideology can only be implemented through the establishment of a truly Islamic state, under the sovereignty of God. The empowerment of Islam, which is God's plan for mankind, is a sacred end. It may be pursued by any means that can be rationalized in terms of Islam's own code. At various times, these have included persuasion, guile, and force.

What is remarkable about fundamentalist Islam is not its diversity. It is the fact that this idea of power for Islam appeals so effectively across such a wide range of humanity, creating a world of thought that crosses all frontiers. Fundamentalists everywhere must act in narrow circumstances of time and place. But they are who they are precisely because their idea exists above all circumstances. Over nearly a century, this idea has evolved into a coherent ideology, which demonstrates a striking consistency in content and form across a wide expanse of the Muslim world.

The Thought of Sayyid al-Afghani

The pursuit of power for Islam first gained some intellectual coherence in the mind and career of Sayyid Jamal al-Din "al-Afghani" (1838–97), a thinker and activist who worked to transform Islam into a lever against Western imperialism. His was an age of European expansion into the heartlands of

Islam, and of a frenzied search by Muslims for ways to ward off foreign conquest. . . .

A contemporary English admirer described Afghani as the leader of Islam's "Liberal religious reform movement." But Afghani—not an Afghan at all, but a Persian who concealed his true identity even from English admirers—was never what he appeared to be. While he called for the removal of some authoritarian Muslim rulers, he ingratiated himself with others. While he had great persuasive power, he did not shrink from conspiracy and violence. A disciple once found him pacing back and forth, shouting: "There is no deliverance except in killing, there is no safety except in killing." These were not idle words. On one occasion, Afghani proposed to a follower that the ruler of Egypt be assassinated, and he did inspire a supple disciple to assassinate a ruling shah of Iran in 1896. Afghani was tempted by power, and believed that "power is never manifested and concrete unless it weakens and subjugates others." Quoting this and other evidence, one Arab critic has argued that there is a striking correspondence between Afghani's thought and European fascism. . . .

Between Afghani and the emergence of full-blown fundamentalism, liberal and secular nationalism would enjoy a long run in the lands of Islam. Europe had irradiated these lands with the idea that language, not religion, defined nations. In the generation that followed Afghani, Muslims with an eye toward Europe preferred to be called Arabs, Turks, and Persians. "If you looked in the right places," wrote the British historian Arnold Toynbee in 1929, "you could doubtless find some old fashioned Islamic Fundamentalists still lingering on. You would also find that their influence was negligible." Yet that same year, an Egyptian schoolteacher named Hasan al-Banna (1906–49) founded a movement he called the Society of the Muslim Brethren. It would grow into the first modern fundamentalist movement in Islam.

Fundamentalists in Egypt and Iran

The Muslim Brethren emerged against the background of growing resentment against foreign domination. The Brethren had a double identity. On one level, they operated openly, as a membership organization of social and political awakening. Banna preached moral revival, and the Muslim Brethren engaged in good works. On another level, however, the Muslim Brethren created a "secret apparatus" that acquired weapons and trained adepts in their use. Some of its guns were deployed against the Zionists in Palestine in 1948, but the Muslim Brethren also resorted to violence in Egypt. They began to enforce their own moral teachings by intimidation, and they initiated attacks against Egypt's Jews. They assassinated judges and struck down a prime minister in 1949. Banna himself was assassinated two months later, probably in revenge. The Muslim Brethren then hovered on the fringes of legality, until Gamal Abdel Nasser, who had survived one of their assassination attempts in 1954, put them down ruthlessly. Yet the Muslim Brethren continued to plan underground and in prison, and they flourished in other Arab countries to which they were dispersed.

At the same time, a smaller and more secretive movement, known as the Devotees of Islam, appeared in Iran, under the leadership of a charismatic theology student, Navvab Safavi (1923–56). Like the Muslim Brethren, the Devotees emerged at a time of growing nationalist mobilization against foreign domination. The group was soon implicated in the assassinations of a prime minister and leading secular intellectuals. The Devotees, who never became a mass party, overplayed their hand and were eventually suppressed. Navvab himself was executed, after inspiring a failed assassination attempt against another prime minister. But the seed was planted. One of those who protested Navvab's execution was an obscure, middle-aged cleric named Ruhollah Khomeini, who would continue the work of forging Islam and resentment into an ideology of power. . . .

Islamic fundamentalists sought to replace weak rulers and states with strong rulers and states. Such a state would have to be based on Islam, and while its precise form remained uncertain, the early fundamentalists knew it should not be a constitutional government or multiparty democracy. . . . This preference for a strong, authoritarian Islamic state, often rationalized by the claim that Islam and democracy are incompatible, would become a trademark of fundamentalist thought and practice.

The pursuit of this strong utopian state often overflowed into violence against weak existing states. These "reformers" were quick to disclaim any link to the violence of their followers, denying that their adepts could read their teachings as instructions or justifications for killing. Afghani set the tone, following the assassination of Iran's shah by his disciple. "Surely it was a good deed to kill this bloodthirsty tyrant," he opined. "As far as I am personally concerned, however, I have no part in this deed." Banna, commenting on the assassinations and bombings done by the Muslim Brethren, claimed that "the only ones responsible for these acts are those who commit them." Navvab, who failed in his one attempt at assassination, sent young disciples in his stead. For years he enjoyed the protection of leading religious figures while actually putting weapons in the hands of assassins. (Only when abroad did he actually boast. "I killed Razmara," he announced on a visit to Egypt in 1954, referring to the prime minister assassinated by a disciple three years earlier.) But despite the denials, violence became the inescapable shadow of fundamentalist Islam from the outset—and the attempt to separate figure from shadow, a problematic enterprise at best.

A Transnational Movement

The fundamentalist forerunners also determined that fundamentalist Islam would have a pan-Islamic bent. The peripatetic Afghani took advantage of steamship and train, crossing political borders and sectarian divides to spread his message of Islamic solidarity. His Paris newspaper circulated far and wide in Islam, through the modern post. Egypt's Muslim Brethren also looked beyond the horizon. In 1948, they sent their own volunteers to fight the Jews in Palestine. Over the next decade, branches of the Muslim Brethren appeared across the Middle East and North Africa, linked by publications and conferences. Egyptian Brethren fleeing arrest set up more branches in Europe, where they mastered the technique of the bank transfer.

The fundamentalist forerunners even laid bridges over the historic moat of Sunni prejudice that surrounded Shi'i Iran. Iran's Devotees of Islam mounted massive demonstrations for Palestine, and recruited 5,000 volunteers to fight Israel. They were not allowed to leave for the front, but Navvab himself flew to Egypt and Jordan in 1953, to solidify his ties with the Muslim Brethren. Visiting the Jordanian-Israeli armistice line, he had to be physically restrained from throwing himself upon the Zionist enemy. Navvab presaged those Iranian volunteers who arrived in Lebanon thirty years later to wage Islamic jihad against Israel.

From the outset, then, fundamentalists scorned the arbitrary boundaries of states, and demonstrated their resolve to think and act across the frontiers that divide Islam. The jet, the cassette, the fax, and the computer network would later help fundamentalists create a global village of ideas and action—not a hierarchical "Islamintern" but a flat "Islaminform"—countering the effects of geographic distance and sectarian loyalty. Not only has the supposed line between "revivalist" and "extremist" been difficult to draw. National and sectarian lines have been erased or smudged, and fundamentalists draw increasingly on a common reservoir for ideas, strategies, and support.

A resolute anti-Westernism, a vision of an authoritarian Islamic state, a propensity to violence, and a pan-Islamic urge: these were the biases of the forerunners of fundamentalist Islam. No subsequent fundamentalist movement could quite shake them. Indeed, several thinkers subsequently turned these biases into a full-fledged ideology. . . .

Iran's Revolution

It was Ruhollah Khomeini (1902–89) who wrote the ideological formula for the first successful fundamentalist revolution in Islam. Khomeini added nothing to fundamentalist ideology by his insistence on the need for an Islamic state, created if necessary by an Islamic revolution, but he made a breakthrough with his claim that only the persons most learned in Islamic law could rule: "Since Islamic government is a government of law, knowledge of the law is necessary for the ruler, as has been laid down in tradition." The ruler "must surpass all others in knowledge," and be "more learned than everyone else." Since no existing state had such a ruler, Khomeini's doctrine constituted an appeal for region-wide revolution, to overturn every extant form of authority and replace it with rule by Islamic jurists. In Iran, where such jurists had maintained their independence from the state all along, this doctrine transformed them into a revolutionary class, bent on the seizure and exercise of power. Much to the astonishment of the world—fundamentalists included—the formula worked, carrying Khomeini and his followers to power on a tidal wave of revolution in 1979. . . .

Khomeini's delegitimation of rule by nominal Muslim kings and presidents found a powerful echo, and he demonstrated how a revolution might succeed in practice. Khomeini also showed how cultural alienation could be translated into a fervid antiforeign sentiment, an essential cement for a broad revolutionary coalition. Later it would be assumed that only "extremists" beyond Iran were thrilled by Iran's revolution. In fact, the enthusiasm among fundamentalists was almost unanimous. As a close reading of the press of the Egyptian Muslim Brethren has demonstrated, even this supposedly sober movement approached the Iranian revolution with "unqualified enthusiasm and unconditional euphoria," coupled with an "uncritical acceptance of both its means and goals." Sunni doubts would arise about implementation of the Islamic state in Iran, but for the next decade, much of the effort of fundamentalists would be invested in attempts to replicate Khomeini's success and bring about a second Islamic revolution.

The attempts to make a second revolution demonstrated that fundamentalists of all kinds would employ revolutionary violence if they thought it would bring them to power. Frustrated by the drudgery of winning mass support, full of the heady ideas of Mawlana Mawdudi and Sayyid Qutb [early twentieth-century fundamentalist revolutionaries], and inspired by Khomeini's success, they lunged forward. From the wild-eyed to the wily, Sunni fundamentalists of all stripes began to conspire. A messianic sect seized the Great Mosque in Mecca in 1979. A group moved by Qutb's teachings assassinated Egyptian President Anwar Sadat in 1981. The Muslim Brethren declared a rebellion against the Syrian regime in 1982. Another path of violence paralleled this one—the work of the half-dozen Shi'i movements in Arab lands that had emerged around the hub of Islamic revolution in Iran. They targeted their rage against the existing order in Iraq, Saudi Arabia, Kuwait, Lebanon, and the smaller Gulf states. In Iraq, they answered Khomeini's appeal by seeking to raise the country's Shi'is in revolt in 1979. In Lebanon, they welcomed Iran's Revolutionary Guards in 1982, first to help drive out the Israelis, then to send suicide bombers to blow up the barracks of U.S. and French peacekeepers there in 1983. Another Shi'i bomber nearly killed the ruler of Kuwait in 1985. Some of Khomeini's adepts went to Mecca as demonstrators, to preach revolution to the assembled pilgrims. Others hijacked airliners and abducted foreigners. Khomeini put a final touch on the decade when he incited his worldwide following to an act of assassination, issuing a religious edict demanding the death of the novelist Salman Rushdie in 1989.

This violence was not an aberration. It was a culmination. From the time of Afghani, fundamentalists had contemplated the possibility of denying power through assassination, and taking power through revolution. Because resort to political violence carried many risks, it had been employed judiciously and almost always surreptitiously, but it remained a legitimate option rooted firmly in the tradition, and it became the preferred option after Iran's revolution emboldened fundamentalists everywhere. For the first time, the ideology of Islam had been empowered, and it had happened through revolution. Power for Islam seemed within reach, if only the fundamentalists were bold enough to run the risk. Many of them were. They included not just the avowed revolutionaries of the Jihad Organization in Egypt, but the cautious and calculating readerships of the Muslim Brethren in Syria and the Shi'i Da'wa Party in Iraq.

It was a seesaw battle throughout the 1980s. Nowhere was Iran's experience repeated. The masses did not ignite in revolution, the rulers did not board jumbo jets for exile. Regimes often employed ruthless force to isolate and stamp out the nests of fundamentalist "sedition." Fundamentalists faced the gaol and the gallows in Egypt. Their blood flowed in the gutters of Hama in Syria, Mecca in Saudi Arabia, and Najaf in Iraq. Yet fundamentalists also struck blows in return, against government officials, intellectuals, minorities, and foreigners. While they did not take power anywhere, they created many semiautonomous pockets of resistance. Some of these pockets were distant from political centers, such as the Bekaa Valley in Lebanon and several governates of Upper Egypt, but fundamentalists also took root in urban quarters and on university campuses, where Islamic dress for women became compulsory and short-cropped beards for men became customary. From time to time, impatient pundits would proclaim that the tide of fundamentalist Islam had gone out, but its appeal obviously ran much deeper. Its straightforward solution to the complex crisis of state and society spoke directly to the poor and the young, the overqualified and the underemployed, whose numbers were always increasing faster than their opportunities.

Ideological Coherence

After Iran's revolution and the subsequent revolts, it was impossible to dismiss the ideological coherence fundamentalist Islam had achieved. It had succeeded in resurrecting in many minds an absolute division between Islam and unbelief. Its adherents, filled with visions of power, had struck at the existing order, turned against foreign culture, and rejected not only apologetics but politics—the pursuit of the possible through compromise. Fundamentalism mobilized its adherents for conflict, for it assumed that the power sought for Islam existed only in a finite quantity. It could only be taken at the expense of others: rulers, foreigners, minorities. Fundamentalists did not admit the sharing of this power, anymore than they admitted the sharing of religious truth, and although fundamentalists differed on the means of taking power, they were unanimous on what should be done with it. One observer has written that even in Egypt, where the fundamentalist scene seemed highly fragmented, the political and social program of the violent fringe groups "did not seem to differ much from that of the mainstream Muslim Brethren," and was shared by "almost the whole spectrum of political Islam." This was true, by and large, for fundamentalist Islam as a whole.

VIEWPOINT 4

"The Muslim Brotherhood dissociates itself
and denounces, without any hesitation, all
forms of violence and terrorism."

Islamic Fundamentalism Does Not Foster Violence in the Middle East

Muhammad M. El-Hodaiby

Muhammad M. El-Hodaiby is a leader of the Muslim Brotherhood in Egypt, an Islamic political organization founded in 1928 (and which has been officially banned by the Egyptian government). In the following viewpoint he maintains that the tenets of Islam uphold justice, human dignity, pluralism, and nonviolence. Misleading Western interpretations of Islamic fundamentalism, he contends, have led many to conclude that Islamic renewal movements are inherently violent—a conclusion El-Hodaiby rejects. Those Muslims who do participate in violence are reacting, in a misguided way, to governmental attempts to suppress Islamic resurgence. In actuality, El-Hodaiby argues, most Islamic revival movements simply aim to help Muslims return to the principles of true Islam.

As you read, consider the following questions:

1. How did Western imperialism affect Muslim societies, in El-Hodaiby's opinion?
2. According to the author, why is "Political Islam" a misleading term?
3. According to the texts of the Koran [Qur'an], cited by El-Hodaiby, what rights do non-Muslims have in Muslim states?

Muhammad M. El-Hodaiby, "Upholding Islam: The Goals of Egypt's Muslim Brotherhood," *Harvard International Review*, Spring 1997. Copyright © 1997 by Harvard International Relations Council, Inc. Reproduced by permission.

Ever since the Egyptian people, along with other African and Asian peoples, embraced Islam in the deep-seated conviction that it is a true religion revealed to a true prophet, Islam has fully characterized the life and activities of those peoples. The two basic sources of Islam—the Holy Qur'an and the *sunna* (authentic traditions of the Prophet)— became the sole reference point for the life of the Muslim individual, family, and community as well as the Muslim state and all economic, social, political, cultural, educational, and legislative and judiciary activities. The Islamic creed and *shari'a* (law) ruled over the individual and society, the ruler and the ruled; neither a ruler nor a ruled people could change anything they prescribed.

Since the Islamic shari'a was revealed by God, judges applied its teachings and fulfilled its rules with no intervention from the rulers. A massive wealth of jurisprudence developed (*fiqh*) from the work of scores of scholars who devoted their lives to the interpretation of the Qur'an and sunna through the use of *ijtihad*, the exercise of independent judgment. Various schools of thought emerged, differing mainly on secondary matters, as well as on some points of application. Believers in religions other than Islam, meanwhile, lived in the Islamic homeland secure in their persons, honor, and property as well as everything they held dear. Except for isolated cases, history does not show Muslim persecution of non-Muslims.

The comprehensive Islamic system remained dominant in the Islamic states. This does not mean that the application was perfectly sound or that the rulers perpetrated no wrongs. In fact, many of the texts were abandoned or incorrectly interpreted. After the first three caliphs who succeeded the Prophet as leader of the Muslim community, disputes arose over the selection of head of state. Internal wars broke out, and the leadership of the state soon changed from a caliphate chosen through shura, a process of consultation, to a hereditary and tyrannical monarchy. This deviation from the tenets of Islam occurred even though the relevant text remained clear and unchanged in the Qur'an. Still, the rulers' tyranny was restricted by the jurisprudence of scholars based on the Qur'an and sunna, which left little room for the rulers to promulgate public laws out of character with the shari'a.

The Colonial Christian Invasion

In the period of colonial Christian invasion, the Islamic shari'a was excluded from serving as the constitution and law of the state. Egypt was occupied by the British in September 1882; less than a year later, in July 1883, Islamic religious courts were replaced by "national courts." Most of the new judges were non-Egyptians, and the law they applied were translated French laws, which became the dominant laws in civil, commercial, and criminal cases. The jurisdiction of Islamic religious courts was restricted to areas of personal status, marriage, divorce, and the related issues of establishing lineage, dowries, and alimonies. The Islamic economic system was replaced by a system of banks, despite the prohibition of the interest rate under Islamic shari'a. In the educational realm, new schools offered few opportunities for the young to learn the creed and tenets of their religion. The social system permitted alcohol, prostitution, gambling, and other activities forbidden in Islam.

The countries and peoples subjected to the armies, creed, and social, economic, and ethical systems of the West struggled for independence. After many years, they managed to regain some of their freedom, but they emerged from the age of imperialism with a weak social structure and a ruined economic system in which poverty, ignorance, disease, and backwardness prevailed. Consequently, the system of government became corrupt and weak. Tyrants emerged that were supported by the forces of imperialism, which withdrew their armies but retained much of their influence.

Since the overwhelming majority of these peoples in Muslim societies believed in Islam and embraced it as a full system of life, forces soon appeared among them that strove to awaken the spirit of faith and remove ideas that had emerged during the decadent era of imperialism. Movements of Islamic revival became active to spread correct Islamic thought and demand the application of the rulings of the Islamic shari'a, particularly the basic principles which ensure shura, freedom, justice, and socioeconomic balance.

Among the strongest of these movements is the Muslim Brotherhood, which originated in Egypt in 1928, during the waning years of military colonialism, and has continued its struggle to the present.

Key Principles of the Muslim Brotherhood

The call of the Muslim Brotherhood was based on two key pillars. First, the Muslim Brotherhood aimed to institute Islamic shari'a as the controlling basis of state and society. About 97 percent of the Egyptian people are Muslims, the majority of whom perform the rites of worship and the ethics enjoined by Islam. But in Egypt, legislation, the judiciary, and economic and social systems are founded on non-Islamic bases. The disjunction between government legislation and policy, on the one hand, and the Islamic shari'a on the other, led to the emergence of many social, economic, and political practices that are invalid under Islamic shari'a. Realizing that a government that is committed to Islam cannot be established without a popular base that believes in its teachings, the Muslim Brotherhood strove to provide a mechanism for the education of society in Islamic principles and ethics.

Second, the Muslim Brotherhood worked to help liberate Muslim countries from foreign imperialism and achieve unity among them, contributing to the struggle against the occupying British armies in Egypt while continuously backing liberation movements in many Arab and Islamic countries. The ruling powers in many of these countries are totalitarian, tyrannical, and personalist, denying popular will and elections, despite the extensive propaganda they finance to convince people otherwise. Because these governments rely on foreign influence, and in view of their special formation and military nature, there have been repeated clashes between them and the Muslim Brotherhood. In Egypt, three years after the assassination in 1949 of Hasan Al-Banna, the founder of the Brotherhood, clashes broke out between the Brotherhood and the military regime. In the era of Gamal Abdel-Nasser, thousands of group leaders and members were arrested, jailed, and tortured; six of the Brotherhood's top leaders were executed by Nasser in 1954 and many others killed in prisons and detention camps. Twelve years later, the famous intellectual Sayyid Qutb and two other leaders were also killed.

After a period of relative calm, the authorities in Egypt resumed their campaign against the Brotherhood. Shortly before the parliamentary elections of 1995, they arrested 62 of the most prominent Brotherhood leaders and brought them before military courts on the pretext of their political activity and preparations for running in elections. Despite these obstacles, the Muslim Brotherhood remains the largest and most effective political and doctrinal movement in Egypt.

Western Media Misinterpretations

In the West the rise of Islamic movements led to attempts, especially in the media, to characterize the nature of Islamic resurgence. The Western media usually tries to relate events in other parts of the world to historical experiences in the West, but their efforts to draw analogies often result in a mixing of fact and fantasy. Among the catch words in the Western media are the misnomer "Islamic fundamentalism" and the misleading term "political Islam."

In the Western experience, religious groups called "fundamentalists" have been characterized by narrow-minded and artificial interpretations of some of their holy books, interpretations which would petrify life and isolate society from thought and culture and even the natural sciences. When Western propaganda and media call some movements of Islamic renewal "fundamentalist," they aim to create a link in the mind of the public between those Islamic movements and the negative connotations of fundamentalism in the West.

As a result, the image of Islamic movements is distorted and their call made repulsive. The fact of the matter is that there is no similarity between the Western notion of fundamentalism and Islamic liberation and renewal movements. The majority of Islamic movements today accept all the exigencies of the modern age, and the natural sciences and technology, unlike the fundamentalisms of the Western experience.

The Western media also speaks of "Political Islam," a misleading term because it gives the false impression that there is a distinction between Islam as a religion, with its creed, rites, and ethics, and Islam as a political system. Groups reflective of political Islam are then seen as falsely attributing to themselves religious sanction in order to gain backing for their political views. But Islam is inherently political: there are categorical texts in the Qur'an making it mandatory to apply the shari'a and act in accordance with it. One verse declares: "O you who believe! Obey God, and obey the Apostle, and those charged with authority among you. If you differ in anything among yourselves, refer it to God and His Apostle, if you do believe in God and the Last Day: that is best, and most suitable for final determination" (Qur'an 4:59). Another one states: "But no, by the Lord, they can have no (real) faith, until they make you judge in all disputes between them, and find in their souls no resistance against your decisions, but accept them with the fullest conviction" (Qur'an 4:65). And there are others.

Shari'a

The teachings of the Islamic shari'a have introduced and regulated the principles of justice, fairness, equality, human dignity, and inviolability of person and property. The shari'a includes texts relating to systems which are now considered to be an integral part of politics. The Muslim Brotherhood demands that these particular shari'a injunctions be implemented. Their enforcement cannot be ignored. Scholars of Al-Azhar University in Cairo, the most important institution specializing in the study of Islam, and the scholars and jurisprudents of all Islamic institutions throughout the world are unanimous in upholding this view.

Muslim scholars are also agreed, however, that no one other than prophets of God are infallible: indeed, the first ruler to come after the Prophet, Abu Bakr Al-Siddiq, came to power saying: "I have become your ruler though I am not the best among you. Obey me as long as I obey God's injunctions regarding you. If I disobey, correct me." Rulers are no more than human beings. Therefore, while the government in Islam is required to abide by the principles of the Islamic shari'a, it is still a civil government that is subject to accountability.

The fixed and unchangeable tenets of the Islamic shari'a are very few, consisting of basic principles designed to achieve justice and social and economic equality, as well as protect human rights, dignity, soul, and property; and preserve and protect the teachings of religion and the system of state. There can always be access to ijtihad to deduce views that are appropriate to global, economic, and social changes. Islam knows no infallible religious government that speaks in the name of God. . . .

A Commitment to Nonviolent Methods

In past years, the Muslim Brotherhood has repeatedly stated that it is involved in political life and has committed itself to legal and nonviolent methods of bringing about change. Its only weapons are honest and truthful words and selfless dedication to social work. In following this course, it is confident that the conscience and awareness of the people are the rightful judges of all intellectual and political trends which compete honestly with one another. Thus, the Muslim Brotherhood reiterates its rejection of any form of violence and coercion as well as all types of coups which destroy the unity of the ummah [nation] because such plots would never give the masses the opportunity to exercise their free will. Furthermore, these methods would create a great crack in the wall of political stability and form an unacceptable assault on the true legitimacy in the society.

Indeed, the present atmosphere of suppression, instability, and anxiety has forced many young men of this nation to commit acts of terrorism which have intimidated innocent citizens and threatened the country's security, as well as its economic and political future. The Muslim Brotherhood dissociates itself and denounces, without any hesitation, all forms of violence and terrorism. In addition, it considers those who shed the blood of others or aid such bloodshed as complicit in sin. Hence, the Brotherhood requests all Muslims to abandon such actions and return to the right way, because "a Muslim is one who refrains from attacking others either physically or verbally." We invite all those who are involved in acts of violence to remember the advice of our Messenger (s.a.w.), in the farewell pilgrimage sermon when he commanded us to protect the sanctity of blood, honor, and property of every Muslim. (Muslims use "s.a.w.," meaning "peace and blessings of God be upon him," after the name of the Prophet).

The Muslim Brotherhood's continuous policy has been one of urging the government not to counter violence with violence, and to abide, instead, by the rules of law and jurisdiction. Some people deliberately and unfairly accuse the Muslim Brotherhood of being involved in terrorist acts. These accusations, stemming from the Brotherhood's unwillingness to support wholeheartedly the confrontational policies of the government, cannot be taken seriously in the light of the clear long-term record of the Muslim Brotherhood's contribution to political life, including its participation in general elections and representative bodies.

The Brotherhood has declared fifteen democratic principles, included in my political program for the November 1995 elections, which we invite all political parties and powers in Egypt to support as a National Charter. These principles declare that "it is not permissible for any one individual, party, group, or institution to claim the right to authority, or to continue in power except with the consent of the people." We upheld the principle "power exchange through free and fair general elections." We confirmed our complete commitment to freedom of religion, opinion, assembly, parliamentary representation and participation (for men and women), an independent judiciary, and an army free from political involvement.

Non-Muslims' Rights

The texts of the Qur'an and sunna obligate Muslims to ensure the safety and security of non-Muslims with revealed books preceding Islam (particularly Jews and Christians) as citizens in the Muslim state. These texts ensure for non-Muslims the freedom of belief and the freedom to abide by the laws in which they believe, not the Islamic shari'a. For example, non-Muslims marry under their own laws, and their marriages are recognized by the Muslim state. Nor are they bound by the dietary laws of Muslims. The Islamic texts allow Muslims to deal with those non-Muslims as long as the

Muslims observe the shari'a in such dealings.

The non-Muslims also have the right to own property, real estate, and all kinds of assets. They can engage in various professions like medicine, engineering, agriculture, and trade. They have the right to assume all offices of state that are not related to enforcing the Islamic shari'a in which they do not believe. In addition, they are free to take their disputes and litigation to competent and knowledgeable persons of their own law. A Muslim judge cannot examine or pass verdicts in these cases unless non-Muslims themselves refer these cases to him.

Islam is Not an Explanation

Islam is not an explanation for the Middle East's uniqueness. Religion is particularly important in the Middle East, and the region is the most autocratic in the world. Yet Islam cannot fully explain these findings; and the disporportionate importance of religion and the presence of autocracy in the region do not lead to the increased levels of ethnic conflict one would expect.

Jonathan Fox, *Middle East Quarterly*, Fall 2001.

The stand of the Muslim Brotherhood is based on the clear Qur'anic edict of no compulsion in religion: we do not wish to compel people to act against their faith or ideology. Our stance regarding our Christian compatriots in Egypt and the Arab world is not new and it is clear and well-known. The Christians are our partners in the country; they were our brothers in the long struggle to liberate the nation. They enjoy all rights of citizenship, financial, psychological, civil, or political. To care for and cooperate with them in every good cause is an Islamic obligation which no Muslim would dare to take lightly.

Honoring Humanity

Today, politicians and thinkers worldwide are raising the banner of pluralism, exhorting recognition of diversity in ideas and actions. However, when the Qur'an was revealed to Prophet Muhammad (s.a.w.) more than 1400 years ago, Islam accepted these differences as universal, and based its political, social, and cultural systems on such variation: "And we made you into nations and tribes, that you may know each other—not that you may depose each other . . ." (Qur'an 49:13). Pluralism according to Islam obliges the recognition of the "other" and requires the psychological and intellectual readiness to accept what truth and good others may possess: as Muslims believe, "wisdom is what a believer should be looking for; wherever he finds it, he should utilize it in the best possible way." Muslims do not hide behind an iron curtain, isolated from relationships with other nations.

The Muslim Brotherhood reaffirms its commitment to this enlightened and wise Islamic viewpoint and reminds all those who follow or quote the Muslim Brotherhood to be sincere in their words and actions. Every Muslim should befriend others and open his heart and mind to everyone, never look down on any person nor remind him of past favors, nor lose patience with him. Brothers' hands should always be extended to others in kindness and love. Their approach to the whole world is one of peace in words and actions, following the example of our Messenger (s.a.w.), a mercy sent to all the worlds. . . .

It is worthwhile to remind ourselves and others that Islam is the only ideological and political system that has honored man and humanity to the utmost degree. Islam is absolutely free from all forms of discrimination, whether based on race, color, or culture. From the beginning Islam has protected the lives, privacy, dignity, and property of all individuals and considered any violation of these sanctities a sin. It has also made their protection a religious duty and an Islamic act of devotion, even if non-Muslims do not follow such standards.

The Qur'an explains this as follows: ". . . And let not the hatred of others make you swerve to wrong and depart from justice. Be just: that is nearer to piety." (Qur'an 5:8). If some Muslims, now or in the past, have not committed themselves to this obligation, their misdeeds should not be attributed to Islam. It has been commonly accepted in writings on the philosophy of Islamic jurisprudence that "you can identify true men by seeing them stick to truth, but truth cannot be identified by seeing those who follow it."

Human Rights

The Muslim Brotherhood would like to proclaim to everyone that we are at the forefront of those who respect and work for human rights. We call for providing all safeguards for these rights, securing them for every human being and facilitating the practice of all liberties within the framework of ethical values and legal limits. We believe that human freedom is the starting point for every good cause, for progress and creativity. The violation of human freedom and rights under any banner, even Islam, is a degradation of man and a demotion from the high position in which God has placed him, and it prevents man from utilizing his initiative and powers to prosper and develop.

At the same time, we present to the world's conscience tragic acts of injustice afflicting those Muslims who have never hurt anyone. It is the duty of all wise men to protest loudly, calling for the universality of human rights and the enjoyment of human freedom on an equal footing. Such equality is the true way toward international and social peace and toward a new world order. This is our faithful testimony, and this is our call in all truth and sincerity. We invite everyone to turn over a new leaf in human and international relations, so that we may enjoy justice, liberty, and peace: "Our Lord! Decide between us and our people in truth for You are the best to decide." Praise be to Allah and His blessings upon Prophet Muhammad.

Periodical Bibliography

The following articles have been selected to supplement the diverse views presented in this chapter.

America	"Islam and Modernity," November 12, 2001.
Anthony Arnove	"Islam's Divided Crescent," *Nation*, July 8, 2002.
Kevin Baker	"The Upside to Radical Islam," *New York Times*, December 15, 2002.
Lisa Beyer	"Roots of Rage," *Time*, October 1, 2001.
Richard W. Bulliet	"The Crisis Within Islam," *Wilson Quarterly*, Winter 2002.
Stephanie Cronin	"Modernity, Power, and Islam in Iran: Reflections on Some Recent Literature," *Middle Eastern Studies*, October 2001.
Economist	"Democracy and Islam," April 17, 1999.
Dexter Filkins	"Can Islamists Run a Democracy?" *New York Times*, November 24, 2002.
Thomas L. Friedman	"An Islamic Reformation," *New York Times*, December 4, 2002.
Francis Fukuyama and Nadav Samin	"Can Any Good Come of Radical Islam?" *Commentary*, September 2002.
Adrian Karatnycky	"It's Not Islam: Muslims Can Be Free and Democractic," *National Review*, December 31, 2002.
Martin Kramer	"Ballots and Bullets: Islamists and the Relentless Drive for Power," *Harvard International Review*, Spring 1997.
Bernard Lewis	"The Revolt of Islam," *New Yorker*, November 19, 2001.
Valentine M. Moghadam	"Islamic Feminism and Its Discontents," *Signs*, Summer 2002.
Soli Ozel	"Islam Takes a Democratic Turn," *New York Times*, November 5, 2002.
Edward W. Said	"A Devil Theory of Islam," *Nation*, August 12, 1996.
Roger Scruton	"Religion of Peace?: Islam, Without the Comforting Cliches," *National Review*, December 31, 2002.
Gabriel Warburg	"Islam and Democracy," *Middle Eastern Studies*, July 1999.
Ibn Warraq	"Islam, the Middle East, and Fascism," *American Atheist*, Autumn 2001.

CHAPTER 3

What Role Should the United States Play in the Middle East?

Chapter Preface

In 1948 the United States became the first country to recognize the newly formed state of Israel. Since then it has been more involved in Middle Eastern affairs than any other country outside the region. This involvement can be seen in several areas. Militarily, the United States has stationed numerous troops and naval forces in and around the region to promote regional stability. When Iraq invaded Kuwait in 1990, the United States provided leadership and more than a half million troops in the subsequent 1991 Persian Gulf war that liberated Kuwait. For twelve years after that conflict America maintained economic sanctions and launched occasional military strikes against Iraq. In March 2003, after months of speaking of the necessity of "regime change" in Iraq, President George W. Bush ordered a concerted military action against that nation.

America has been heavily involved in the region in ways besides war. Much of the U.S. foreign aid budget goes to countries in the Middle East. Israel, which receives $3 billion in military and economic assistance, and Egypt, which receives $2 billion, lead the world in receiving American aid. Diplomatically, U.S. leaders have historically been heavily involved in peace efforts in the region, with special attention directed to the Arab-Israeli conflict. President Jimmy Carter's involvement was crucial in creating the 1978 peace agreement between Israel and Egypt, for example.

Many analysts identify two primary reasons for America's interest in the Middle East: oil and Israel. America is the world's largest importer of oil and has dwindling domestic reserves. The Middle East nations of Iran, Iraq, Kuwait, Qatar, Saudi Arabia, and the United Arab Emirates contain 65 percent of the world's proven oil reserves and account for 40 percent of the world's crude oil trade. The 1973 oil embargo, in which Saudi Arabia and other countries withheld their oil from the United States, sharply raised oil prices and demonstrated the potential power of Middle Eastern countries to dominate the world oil market in ways detrimental to the United States and other consumer nations. Much U.S. foreign policy is designed to maintain friendly relations with Saudi Arabia and other countries in the region to ensure a stable supply of oil.

While America's interest in oil is based on economics, its support of Israel is based on historical, moral, and geopolitical concerns. After the Holocaust, in which millions of Jews were killed by Nazi Germany during World War II, many Americans supported the Jews' desire for a homeland in the Middle East, which was seen as one way to prevent future Jewish persecution. In addition, Israel is, in the words of political analyst Alon Ben-Meir, "the only democracy in an inherently unstable region," thus providing the United States with a strategic military ally in the Middle East.

These two objectives—a stable oil supply and support of Israel—are often in conflict. American attempts to cultivate good relations with oil-rich Arab states have been complicated by the United States's support of Israel, a country that many Arab states view as an enemy. Because of these conflicts of interest, many commentators argue about whether America is fair in how it treats the opposing parties in the Arab-Israeli conflict. The viewpoints in this chapter debate these and other issues pertaining to U.S. foreign policy in the Middle East.

> "*Because outside intervention [to resolve the Palestinian-Israel conflict] is required, the only superpower capable of orchestrating it successfully is the United States.*"

The United States Should Intervene to End the Israeli-Palestinian Conflict

Sherwin Wine

Rabbi Sherwin Wine is a founder of the Society for Humanistic Judaism and the author of several books including *Judaism Beyond God*. In the following viewpoint he argues that the United States should take an active role in ending the endemic violence between Israelis and Palestinians, which he categorizes as a clash between Jewish and Arab nationalism. He argues that the ongoing conflict between Israelis and Palestinians is not only harming the people of the Middle East but is threatening the global economy. The conflict is so bitter and entrenched that outside intervention is required to end it, he asserts, and only the United States is powerful enough to do so.

As you read, consider the following questions:

1. What is the foundation of the war in Israel, according to Wine?
2. Why do both sides see themselves as victims, according to the author?
3. What elements of an imposed truce settlement does Wine outline?

Sherwin Wine, "Arabs and Jews," *Humanist*, vol. 62, September/October 2002, pp. 15–18. Copyright © 2002 by the American Humanist Association. Reproduced by permission.

The war between the Jews and the Arabs in former British Palestine has been going on for eighty-one years. In 1921, the first Arab explosion against the Zionist pioneers announced the beginning of the fray. Hatred and suspicion have undermined any successful resolution of the conflict.

After the Jewish War of Independence in 1948, the conflict became a war between the Jewish state and external Arab enemies. In that conflict, the Israelis were generally victorious. The Israeli triumph in 1967 crushed Gamal Abdel Nasser, the hero of Arab nationalism. But in 1987 the Palestinian Arabs chose a new kind of battle—internal rebellion. The infitada was born. And it has grown in fury ever since.

Zionist and Arab Nationalism

The foundation of the war is the power of nationalism. Jewish nationalism was born out of the defiance of the oppressed masses in czarist Russia. It was fed by racial anti-Semitism. Diaspora nationalism sought to liberate the Jews of eastern Europe and give them cultural autonomy. It was destroyed by native resistance and the Holocaust.

Zionist nationalism also saw itself as a national liberation movement. It naively proposed to solve anti-Semitism by returning the Jews to their ancient homeland. Reinforced by socialist idealism and the revival of Hebrew as a popular language, it led to the establishment of a Jewish settlement in Palestine. The closing of the doors to immigration in the United States, the support of the British government, and the rise of Adolf Hitler gave this nationalism the impetus that the slaughter of six million Jews was to make irresistible. Zionism became the most powerful movement to mobilize the Jewish masses in the twentieth century.

Arab nationalism was an import from the West and was cultivated initially by Christian Arabs as a way of countering their exclusion by Muslims. Propelled by Turkish oppression and by the humiliation of European conquest, the Arab nationalist movement was led by Westernized intellectuals who embraced secular values and placed nationhood above religion. Since the Arab world never fully experienced the secular revolution which had transformed European life, the Arab nationalism of the street had difficulty distinguishing between Arab loyalty and Muslim loyalty. Religion is inevitably part of the nationalist package in the Muslim world.

Since the Arab world is vast, divided by regional differences, cultural diversity, and the internal boundaries of twenty-two states created by colonial masters, the unification of the Arab nation hasn't been easy. Nasser tried and failed. He was defeated by both the Israelis and by the hostility of his political enemies and rivals within the Arab world.

The one issue that has the power to transcend the internal state boundaries of the Arab world and to mobilize the Arab masses is Zionism. Whether or not it deserves such designation, the Jewish state has become the symbol of Arab humiliation. Perceived as the last and most outrageous example of European colonialism, Israel is the object of almost universal Arab hate. The defeat of Israel has become the ultimate perceived means of restoring Arab honor. The hatred of Zionism is so intense that it is difficult for most Arabs to distinguish between their hostility to Israel and their hatred for Jews.

In fact, the suspicion and hatred between Arabs and Jews is so fierce that dialogue is condemned to failure. Most public and private encounters between conventional Arab and Jewish leaders degenerate into shouting matches. Each side insists on its rights. And, of course, both sides are "right." The Palestinian Arabs have been invaded, abused, and oppressed. The Israeli Jews are by now mainly native-born residents of the land they defend and the creators of a dynamic, modern, high-tech state; they have no place else to go.

From the Jewish point of view, the Arab hostility cannot easily be distinguished from anti-Semitism. The memories of the Holocaust hover over every response. Of course, the popular media in the Arab world reinforce this perception by aping the propaganda of European Jew hatred. From the perspective of the Arabs, Jewish voices are confused with the voices of Jewish extremists who advocate expulsion and deportation.

Extremists and Victims on Both Sides

There is an abundance of extremists on both sides. The Arab and Palestinian nationalist and fundamentalist worlds feature many militant groups that advocate terrorism and call for the destruction of the Jewish state. The Jewish and Israeli extremists are equally militant in their refusal to recognize the right of a Palestinian state to exist (beyond suggesting that Jordan is already a Palestinian state). To the credit of the Israelis, Israel features a peace movement that has no counterpart in the Arab world.

Both sides see themselves as victims. Jews see Israel as a small beleaguered state in a vast and petroleum-rich Arab world that does nothing to rescue its Palestinian brothers and sisters from poverty. Arabs see Israel as the agent of American imperialism, supported by the wealth and military technology of the world's only superpower—a nation that is beholden to Jewish political power.

What President George W. Bush Should Do

The president's basic approach to the Middle East is correct. He is horrified by the suicide bombings and understands Israel's need to respond to them. He also believes, however, that only a political settlement will resolve the problem. He endorses a Palestinian state and has announced an international conference to begin talking about all this. But words mean nothing in the Middle East. . . . The president must aggressively use his power and prestige—his political capital—to push the Palestinians, Israelis and Arabs toward substantive political talks. This is not going to bring peace tomorrow, but it might well lower the tensions, which is good for them—and for the United States.

Fareed Zakaria, *Newsweek*, May 20, 2002.

The failure of the Oslo peace process [a series of peace agreements reached between Israel and the Palestinians in the 1990s] is as much the result of intense hatred and suspicion as it is the incompatibility of vested interests. The issues of boundaries, Jerusalem, and refugees are shrouded by such levels of distrust that the normal compromises that negotiations bring can never emerge. No arrangements can provide the security that most Israelis want. And no "deal" can yield the sense of honor and vindication that most Palestinians and Arabs seek.

In searching for alternatives to endless war, certain realities need to be confronted. This war is not only bad for the Israelis and the Palestinians but also for Jews and Arabs. For the Jews, the war has already spread to Europe, where Muslim militants assault synagogues and vulnerable Jews. For the Arabs, the war prevents any real confrontation with the political, economic, and social issues that affect their world. War continues to justify government by military dictators.

This war is bad for the United States and the rest of the world. The Palestinian issue has provided the fuel whereby Muslim militants have won the allegiance of millions of Arabs and Muslims in their desire to wage war against the United States and Western culture. A war between the West and Islam is a world war. It is different from a war against Muslim fundamentalist terrorism; such a conflict would enjoy the support of most Muslim governments. The success of the United States' response to the attacks of September 11, 2001, lies in the ability to make such a distinction.

A Cycle of Vengeance

Jews and Arabs, Israelis and Palestinians by themselves cannot achieve peace—or even an effective truce—by relying on negotiations alone; the cycle of vengeance has its own logic. Every terrorist action incites retaliation; every retaliation incites counter-retaliation. No antagonist can allow itself to be seen as weak. Revenge is a necessary tactic in maintaining credibility. The cycle cannot stop itself without outside intervention.

The proposed Palestinian state [in 2000 and 2001 negotiations] is no more than 3,000 square miles in size—hardly a formula for viability. It is presently a series of urban "doughnut holes" within Israeli-occupied territory. The presence of the Israeli army is justified not only by the argument for security but also by the necessity to defend small Jewish settlements which have been established in the West Bank and Gaza by religious Jewish settlers laying claim to the land. These settlements prevent peace, add nothing to the security of Israel, and provide more provocation to Arabs to kill more Jews.

Jerusalem is already divided. Jewish Jerusalem (about two-thirds of the expanded city) has no Arabs, while Arab Jerusalem (the eastern sector) has no Jews. While some Arabs work in Jewish Jerusalem, almost no Jews even penetrate Arab Jerusalem unless they are on military duty. A unified city is more desirable than a divided city, but the division already exists.

A binational Israeli-Palestinian state—a dream of many peaceniks—is not politically viable even though it would be economically desirable. Jewish and Arab nationalism are realities; they cannot be wished away. Mutual hatred and suspicion are realities; they cannot be dismissed. Arguing against nationalism may work a hundred years from now but it doesn't fly today. A Jewish state—in which Jewish national culture is the dominant culture and most people speak Hebrew—is no more racist than would be an Arab state whose dominant culture and language reflected its people. Three million Palestinian refugees cannot return to the Jewish state without destroying the Jewish national character of the Jewish state.

U.S. Intervention

Because outside intervention is required, the only superpower capable of orchestrating it successfully is the United States. Since September 11, George W. Bush has mobilized an effective coalition of world powers, including Europe, Russia, China, and India—as well as many allies in the Muslim world. The war between the Israelis and the Palestinians has begun to undermine the coalition, especially with Bush's perceived support of the Ariel Sharon government in Israel. Joint intervention with the approval of the United Nations and with the support of moderate Muslim powers could restore the coalition. This intervention is no different from the intervention that the United States initiated in Bosnia and Kosovo [during their wars in the 1990s].

What would be the elements of such an intervention? The United States controls the process. The Israelis don't trust the United Nations and won't cooperate with an effort managed by the hostile nations of the developing world.

The United States acts as a neutral "parent." It doesn't always praise one side and condemn the other; it creates a setting for negotiations, with the presence of major members of the coalition. The format of such negotiations is only a pretense. In the "back room" the United States dictates the settlement and everybody knows that the United States has imposed the settlement. Both antagonists protest, but they yield because they have no choice. The imposition gives the leaders of both sides an excuse, a way to save face, and a scapegoat. They can justify their "surrender" to their constituencies by pleading helplessness. They may even shake hands reluctantly. Whether [Palestinian leader Yasser] Arafat will still be representing the Palestinians is the question.

All that can realistically be achieved at this time is an effective truce. Peace will have to await a reduction in the fury of hatred and suspicion. For now, an imposed settlement should include the following:

- the removal of all Jewish settlements from the West Bank and Gaza, except those settlements which function as contiguous communities for Tel Aviv and Jerusalem
- the digging of a ditch and construction of a fence between the Jews and Arabs along the adjusted 1967 boundaries
- the policing of this fence by the United States and its European allies
- the granting of Arab East Jerusalem to the Palestinians as their national capital
- the demilitarization of the new Palestinian state, with periodic inspections by the United States and its coalition partners
- compensation for Palestinian refugees who cannot return.

Such compensation may cost over $30 billion and would be covered by the United States, Japan, and European allies. If the compensation helps to bring about an effective truce, it would be worth the investment. Rescuing the global economy for peace justifies the expense.

Compensating Israel

Israel needs to be compensated for its "willingness" to shrink and to confront the wrath of its right-wing extremists. Since it won't in the foreseeable future be accepted by the Arab and Muslim worlds, it needs to be regarded as the European power it is. Israel's high-tech economy needs the European market, just as its European culture needs a European support system. The price that Europe pays for this necessary peace is that it accepts Israel as a member of the European Union. Such acceptance is no different than acceptance of Cyprus or Turkey, and Israelis will be better off trading in euros than shekels.

After this settlement is imposed, terrorist violence will likely continue. The war against Muslim fundamentalist terrorists will also continue. For the extremists in the Arab and Muslim world—and even in the Jewish world—hatred is a way of life. For moderates, an effective truce will enable them to join the forces of peace.

The ball is in Bush's court if he would only lead the way. The leaders of the Defense Department and the religious right will likely oppose this kind of proposal, but only such action can provide any light at the end of the tunnel that is the Middle East.

> "The task of advancing confidence-building measures should be left to the Israelis and Palestinians, and other players in the region."

The United States Should Not Intervene to End the Israeli-Palestinian Conflict

Leon T. Hadar

Leon T. Hadar is the Washington bureau chief of the *Business Times* of Singapore and an adjunct professor at American University in Washington, D.C. His writings include the book *Quagmire: America in the Middle East*. In the following viewpoint he asserts that the United States should not interject itself into the Israeli-Palestinian dispute, arguing that America can do little to alter the dynamics of the conflict. It is up to the Israelis and Palestinians themselves to come up with the necessary compromises to secure peace, he concludes.

As you read, consider the following questions:
1. What actions by Israeli and Palestinian leaders led Hadar to conclude they do not want peace?
2. What harms would result from U.S. efforts to encourage negotiations in the Middle East, according to the author?
3. What steps does Hadar recommend that America take?

The acceptance by Israel and the Palestinian Authority of the cease-fire plan put forth by CIA Director George Tenet [in 2001], has strengthened the hands of those at home and abroad who are arguing that a more-energized diplomatic role by the United States could help end the violence in the Middle East.

American pundits and US allies hope the White House is abandoning its posture of "benign neglect" toward the Israeli-Palestinian conflict, and is ready to adopt the more central role that previous administrations had played in trying to make peace between Arabs and Jews. More specifically, they are urging Washington to press the Israelis and Palestinians to implement the recommendations of the international commission headed by former Sen. George Mitchell, which called for the introduction of "confidence building" steps— including a freeze on the building of new Israeli settlements in the occupied territories, and an effort by Palestinian security forces to end anti-Israeli violence.

A Difference Between Expectations and Reality

But the fact that both sides have accepted the conclusions of the Mitchell report, and may be willing to back a fragile cease-fire brokered by the United States, reflects nothing more than short-term tactics by Israeli and Palestinian officials hoping to win brownie points with Washington and the "international community." That the Israelis and Palestinians cannot reconcile their opposing views on what constitutes "peace," and continue to engage in acts of violence, highlights the wide divergence between the expectations for diplomatic momentum among "peace processing" experts in Washington and the harsh political realities in the Middle East. It demonstrates why the Bush administration should resist the pressure for a new American-led "peace initiative."

Indeed, the election of ultra-nationalist Ariel Sharon as prime minister and the growing militancy on the Palestinian side, where Yasser Arafat seems unwilling or unable to put an end to the intifada, have been clear indications that there is no political support among the leaders and the people involved in this bloody ethnic and religious war for the kind of confidence-building measures proposed by the Mitchell commission.

If anything, Mr. Sharon is intent on increasing the number of Jewish settlers in the West Bank. He is confident that Israel's military power will force the Palestinians to bow to its dictates and give up their demand for full independence. Meanwhile, Arafat is strengthening his alliance with radical Islamic fighters, and hoping the growing violence will trigger a dramatic international response that would leave Washington no choice but to pressure Israel to withdraw from the West Bank and Gaza. Neither side will be willing to modify its position as long as it enjoys domestic support.

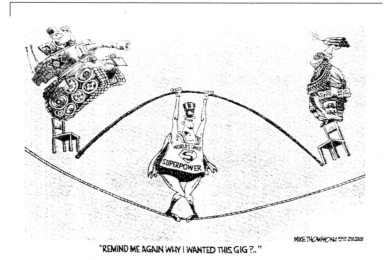

"REMIND ME AGAIN WHY I WANTED THIS GIG?.."

MIKE THOMPSON

Thompson. © 2002 by Copley News Service. Reproduced by permission.

In that context, there is little that Washington could do to change these long-term strategic calculations. A new US effort to energize the "peace process" would only raise expectations among the Palestinians and the other Arabs that President [George W.] Bush could compel Israel to end its settlement policy. But the pro-Israeli disposition in Washington coupled with a weak Arab diplomatic hand make that an unlikely scenario. And the image of a US administration unable to force a change in the repressive Israeli policies would damage America's position in the Arab world, and strengthen Sharon.

Resisting the Interventionist Urge

By resisting the interventionist urge and encouraging the "localization" of the Palestinian-Israeli issue, the Bush administration will send a clear signal to the Palestinians that their only chance of winning political independence is through direct negotiations with the Israelis. Instead of complaining about US diplomatic passivity, Egypt, Jordan, and the European Union should use their power to persuade Arafat to end the violence.

At the same time, Mr. Bush could follow the footsteps of his father's administration by cutting economic aid to Israel by the amount of money it spends on the Jewish settlements in the occupied territories. He could make any continuing military aid to Israel conditional on its agreement to stop using American-made weapons against civilians in the occupied territories.

The task of advancing confidence-building measures should be left to the Israelis and Palestinians, and other players in the region. A successful outcome of such a process could encourage the United States to strengthen its diplomatic and economic ties with them. But Washington should not use its resources to promote such a strategy, so it will not have to pay the costs of its possible failure.

107

VIEWPOINT 3

*"Americans hope for constitutional
governments in the Middle East not
because we are naive, but because we seek
democracy's practical dividends."*

The United States Should
Promote Democratic Regimes
in the Middle East

Victor Davis Hanson

In 2002, when this article was originally published, the United
States was engaged in debate on whether to use military action to effect a "regime change" in Iraq, a country suspected
of hiding weapons of mass destruction. Some proponents of
American military intervention, assuming that it would result
in victory and temporary American occupation of Iraq, argued
that such a course of events could well begin a new era in the
Middle East. In the following viewpoint Victor Davis Hanson
argues that the United States should seize the opportunity
that military intervention in Iraq would provide to promote
democracy in the Middle East. America's past policy of supporting autocratic Middle East regimes in the name of stability, he asserts, has resulted in endemic conflict, human rights
abuses, and anti-American sentiment. Hanson, a professor of
classics at California State University in Fresno, is the author
of several books on military history.

As you read, consider the following questions:

1. What are the practical dividends of democracy in the
   Middle East, according to Hanson?
2. What past examples of U.S. democracy promotion and
   creation does the author cite?

What will our invasion of Iraq unleash? Our greatest challenge may be not the elimination of Iraq's weapons of mass destruction but the subsequent reconfiguration of the Middle East. What happens inside Iraq on the day [Iraqi leader] Saddam Hussein is gone will reveal American intentions, capabilities, and morality. What we do in Iraq will set the stage for success or failure in the entire region.

If we are to promote some quasi-democracy in post-Saddam Iraq, how will we do it? Iraq is a Muslim country with no tradition of consensual government or even an indigenous vocabulary for "democracy," "citizen," "secularism," or "referendum." The realists remind us that the seeds of constitutional government do not grow in soil that lacks a middle class and the rule of law. They point out that there has never been a truly free Arab democracy in 1,500 years. They are joined by the multicultural, moral relativist, and increasingly isolationist Left, which contends that we have no business dictating to any country the nature of its government.

Perhaps, then, we should allow Iraq to lapse into a purportedly pro-American despotism like Saudi Arabia and Egypt—permit some general, say, like [Pervez] Musharraf of Pakistan, to rise to power on promises to pump oil, rein in terrorists, curb the madrassas [religious schools that promote radical Islam], not threaten his neighbors, and reform at some future date. Or perhaps, if the postwar chaos grows overwhelming, we should do as we did in Afghanistan years ago—shrug, declare a victory of sorts, leave quietly, and hope that the feuding Shiites, Kurds, Baathists, and generals we leave behind turn out to be better and weaker than Saddam Hussein.

Conflicting advice comes daily from all sides, from Middle Eastern dissidents, Arabists, Islamic diplomats, and the Europeans. But we should decide for ourselves upon a course of action before we go to Iraq. If we profess support for democracy in Iraq now, before the bombs fall, this assurance to the Iraqi people may help our cause more than a European armored division or a Middle Eastern base. Our commitment to political reform—not to any individual or clique—will give us the military and ethical advantage of consistency, purpose, and clarity.

Americans hope for constitutional governments in the Middle East not because we are naive, but because we seek democracy's practical dividends. Modern democracies rarely attack America or each other. When they fight illiberal regimes, they win. The Falklands, Panama, Serbia, and the Middle East all demonstrate the power of legitimate governments over dictatorships. Yet this pragmatic consideration is often dismissed as starry-eyed idealism. Only belatedly have we advocated democratic reform for the Palestinians, as a remedy for our previous failed policy of appeasement of [Yasser] Arafat and his corrupt regime.

We are not talking of Jeffersonian democracy all at once. First, remove the dictator, to permit a more lawful society to evolve on the model of Panama, Grenada, Serbia, and the Philippines. Keep up the pressure of American and world opinion, international aid, the return of Westernized dissidents, the emancipation of women, and the occasional threat of American force. Let [the September 11, 2001, terrorist attacks] remind us that inaction can be as deadly as intervention.

Two Converging Camps

In the past, Americans were told that the Middle East was divided roughly into two camps (plus democratic Israel): the sometime sponsors of terror (Afghanistan, Algeria, Iran, Iraq, Lebanon, Libya, Syria, and Yemen) and the so-called moderate dictatorships (Egypt, the Gulf states, Jordan, Morocco, Saudi Arabia, and Tunisia). Although the latter group ruled without a popular mandate and made use of coercion and intimidation, they nevertheless curbed their brutality and either condemned or ignored but did not openly abet terrorists.

Our State Department has the unenviable task of maintaining workable relationships with these allegedly pro-Western regimes—at a time when some friends and foes are looking more and more alike. Lunatic Iran still pumps oil; the sober Saudis murmur of boycotts. Saudis in the United States are enraged at us; Iraqis living here lobby congressmen to liberate their country. Our tanks and planes can obliterate armies, but they can't stop suicide-murderers. Washington may assure us that Egypt and Saudi Arabia are our friends, yet their citizens comprise the majority of the September 11 terrorists and the detainees at Guantanamo—while Libyans, Syrians, and Iraqis are less likely to join al Qaeda.[1]

The events of the last year [2001] prove that both extremist and moderate governments in the Middle East are riding a tidal wave of resentment. Governments of both kinds seek to survive largely through bribery, oppression, and censorship, and by scapegoating Israel and America. This they hope will postpone an accounting with their people. In the absence of elections, free speech, or any public audit of government finances, our "friends" must divert the attention of their restless populations to the bogeyman of the West. Yet at root, the Arab masses probably hate us less than they abhor their own governments for lack of freedom and economic progress. If Islamic zeal were the cure for what ails these regimes, Saudi Arabia, Pakistan, and Iran would be pillars of stability.

Middle East Pathologies

The pathologies of the Middle East are urgent and will only get worse if left alone. The last two decades of ruined economies have brought nothing but disaster. The unusually candid "Arab Human Development Report 2002," issued by leading Arab intellectuals under the auspices of the United Nations, provides the details. An exploding population (38 percent is under 14 years of age) will have to fight for scarce resources: The 22 Arab countries have a combined gross domestic product less than Spain's. The wealthiest 85,000 Saudi families have overseas assets of $700 billion. Labor productivity fell between 1960 and 1990, while it soared elsewhere. Even Africa outperformed the Arab world in rates of economic growth and the incidence of constitutional government between 1975 and 1990. More foreign books were translated into Greek than into Arabic [in 2001]. The report speculates that half the youths in most Arab countries desire to emigrate—usually to the lands of the infidels, Europe or the United States.

In response to this depressing state of affairs, an exasper-

---

1. Al Qaeda is the terrorist network believed responsible for the September 11, 2001, terrorist attacks on America. Following America's subsequent military response in Afghanistan, where al Qaeda was headquartered, hundreds of suspected al Qaeda members were taken to America's naval base in Guantanamo Bay, Cuba.

ated United States has tried everything from appeasement to confrontation—everything except systematic, sustained, and unqualified support for democratic reform. On that score, our experience in Afghanistan is encouraging. [In 2001], no country in the Middle East was more lawless, anti-American, or brutal than Afghanistan under the Taliban [Afghanistan's former ruling regime]; today, our intervention has produced a more consensual government, and refugees are going home. A secular and democratic Turkey, meanwhile, proves that Islam is not intrinsically incompatible with liberal society. And reforms in Qatar promise hope for eventual elections; Qatar's liberality explains the absence of a Saudi-style backlash from the populace, as well as the regime's willingness to work with us on energy and defense.

The "realist" rejoinder is that elections in the Middle East are a onetime thing. In Iran, the ouster of the autocratic shah made way for an election, after which the mullahs destroyed democracy; Khomeini's death only brought in more fanatics.[2] Arafat rigged an election and hasn't held another. Jordan's parliament is a façade behind which King Abdullah rules by kowtowing to Iraq, Syria, the Palestinians, and the United States. The very idea of elections brought disaster in Algeria.

Yet even these dismal scenarios are instructive. The fact that the mullahs were elected in Iran has put an enormous burden of legitimacy upon them; their abject failure may better serve the long-term interests of the United States than the Saudi royal family's success. Palestinians too are talking more about the need for fair elections than the need to keep Arafat in office. America has much to gain when democracy works, while autocratic regimes profess stability but are volatile under the surface. Better to deal with a subverted democracy: At least its people will soon realize that they, not the United States, are responsible for their disasters.

Limits of Realpolitik

The problem with the old realpolitik is not just that it is occasionally amoral but also that it has been tried and found

---

2. Ayatollah Ruhollah Khomeini, the leader of Iran's 1979 Islamic Revolution, died in 1989.

wanting. Short-term stability has left unaddressed the festering long-term problem of Arab development. The rot now overwhelms us.

Ending the Democratic Exception

The United States does play a large role on the world stage, and our efforts to promote democracy throughout the Muslim world have sometimes been halting and incomplete. Indeed, in many parts of the Muslim world, and particularly in the Arab world, successive U.S. administrations, Republican and Democratic alike, have not made democratization a sufficient priority.

At times, the United States has avoided scrutinizing the internal workings of countries in the interests of ensuring a steady flow of oil, containing Soviet, Iraqi and Iranian expansionism, addressing issues related to the Arab-Israeli conflict, . . . or securing basing rights for our military. Yet by failing to help foster gradual paths to democratization in many of our important relationships—by creating what might be called a "democratic exception"—we missed an opportunity to help these countries become more stable, more prosperous, more peaceful, and more adaptable to the stresses of a globalizing world.

It is not in our interest—or that of the people living in the Muslim world—for the United States to continue this exception. U.S. policy will be more actively engaged in supporting democratic trends in the Muslim world than ever before.

Richard N. Haas, address before the Council on Foreign Relations, December 4, 2002.

We must try something new, out of self-interest. We need to prevent more Egyptians, Kuwaitis, Pakistanis, Palestinians, and Saudis from murdering more Americans, as their "shocked," subsidized, and protected governments shrug, send condolences, and remind us that their "friendship" should earn them immunity from U.S. bombs. The world is not static. What worked for the last fifty years—a mixture of concern for oil, opposition to communism, and profits from weapons sales—no longer justifies supporting duplicitous dictators who can scarcely feed their own people in a region awash in petroleum. The end of Soviet-sponsored communism means we no longer need fear that elected socialists will turn into Communist props.

We cannot continue to treat symptoms rather than the etiology of the disease. We have used restrained military force to send a message to the occasional megalomaniac who boasted of killing Americans. So we bombed [Libyan leader Muammar] Qaddafi; blasted the Sudanese; sent cruise missiles into Afghan caves; shelled Lebanon; and hit Iraq in the no-fly zones.[3] It was a tit-for-tat strategy, originated by [former president Ronald] Reagan, institutionalized by the elder Bush [former president George Bush], and popularized by [former president Bill] Clinton.

The advantage of a reactive strategy seemed to be that it let Americans go on living without much disruption or cost in lives and treasure. But September 11 taught us otherwise: The terrorists and their hosts saw that we offered no sustained threat to their operations, and they seized their chance. Now, they will not be content with blowing up an embassy or a ship. They deal in symbols and shock, and so will always, like carnival barkers or professional wrestlers, be seeking to meet or exceed their prior achievements.

A New Strategy

The alternative to the old realpolitik is a brand new strategy oriented toward ending the entire apparatus of autocracy and creating in its place the conditions for future political legitimacy and economic growth in the Middle East. Rather than fearing the uncertainty that this would entail, we should understand that sometimes temporary chaos may be better than enduring stasis.

Indeed, this is the course on which we have embarked in Afghanistan—as revolutionaries of sorts, rather than Pollyanna interventionists or cynical isolationists. The verdict is still out on the stability of the [Homid] Karzai government, much less the country's long-term prospects. Clearly, though, the present government gives Afghanistan its first ray of hope

---

3. Following the 1991 Gulf War, the United States, Great Britain, and France imposed no-fly zones in northern and southern parts of Iraq. Iraqi aircraft are forbidden to operate in these areas, ostensibly to protect ethnic and religious groups from Iraqi persecution. The United States and Great Britain have since enforced these zones through bombing missions against Iraqi air defense targets.

in three decades. Before September 11, Pakistan was considered a humane place compared with Afghanistan; now the Karzai government arguably holds more promise than Musharraf's dictatorship. And yet under American pressure, Pakistan today offers some improvement over a year ago, when we largely ignored its anti-democratic pathologies. Could the nascent, legitimate Afghanistan—backed by American and European aid, the return of dissidents and exiles from the West, an influx of social workers, the emancipation of women, the establishment of schools, and the threat of force—offer hope elsewhere in the Middle East?

History provides more encouragement than we might think. Cynics in 1945 warned us that Japanese terrorists would make an American occupation of mainland Japan impossible. The traditions of Japan were Asian and authoritarian, they said, and we should not confuse a desire for Western weapons and industry with any capacity for democracy. Yet we plunged in, and in five years Japan had become the sanest and most humane society between San Francisco and Beijing. Rather than search for a Westernized leader, we took on the greater burden of establishing institutions in a completely foreign landscape. Simultaneously, Germany and Italy, both historically unstable republics, were transmogrified from fascist killer states into liberal republics almost overnight.

We poured in aid, brought their rehabilitated governments into the world community, interfered with their school systems, empowered women, stationed troops to monitor recidivism, sought out moderates, dissidents, and exiles, helped to draft constitutions, tried the guilty—then crossed our fingers that the people's inclusion in decision-making and enjoyment of personal freedom would bring a new maturity and responsibility to society. Today, without the specter of a global and nuclear Soviet Union to make "regime change" difficult and distort elections, we are once again free to promote democracy in unlikely places.

There are now millions of exiles from the Middle East residing in Western countries who want Western liberalism to take root in their native lands. Democracy has no rival in French Marxism, Communist nostalgia, or Baathist nonsense. Unlike communism, Islamic fundamentalism does not even purport to bring progress and equality. Nor has it a nuclear patron with global reach, like the old Soviet Union. We need not fear a universal Islamic fundamentalism. It may thrive in Saudi Arabia, where fanaticism of one sort or another is the only way to foment revolution, but it has alienated the masses in theocratic Iran, now that the extremists have lost the romance of tormented idealists and are seen as accountable for their institutionalized oppression. We also have an ally in global popular culture. However crass, free expression subverts theocracy and dictatorship.

Costs and Dangers

We must not be naive. Establishing lawful rule in lawless places entails real costs and dangers. Thus, war or the threat of force may be the necessary catalyst. Germany and Japan did not abandon fascism voluntarily. . . . Armed resistance can bring profound change because defeat brings humiliation, and humiliation sometimes precipitates a collective change of heart. The Eastern Europeans, and eventually the Russians, broke free because they saw the Soviet Union was exhausted, had lost the Cold War, and was near collapse. When the generals and colonels of Greece and Argentina brought military ruin and embarrassment to their countries, they fled. South Korea and Taiwan were born out of war; they survived and eventually democratized because America vowed to protect them with force.

In the Middle East, there will be no change until Saddam Hussein is defeated and what he stands for is shown to lead only to oblivion. The use of military power must be decisive, producing a rout, not a stalemate. Were we to intervene and then hesitate or otherwise lose, we might achieve the opposite result from that desired—encouraging strongmen to "stand up to" the United States.

A second price we must be willing to pay is the lengthy presence of American troops. They are still in Germany, Italy, Japan, and South Korea. All that prevents the violent overthrow of democracies in Latin America and their replacement with dictatorships is fear of the Marines. Taiwan remains free only because of the proximity of American carriers and submarines. We already have thousands of soldiers in the Gulf states and Saudi Arabia: They could just as well protect democracies as keep a watch on or support tyrants.

A third burden we must assume is that we must expect and not fear anti-Americanism. Newly created democracies will not necessarily love us. Look at postwar France, which resented the United States mere months after it was liberated. Arabs may feel some identification with Europe, given their former colonial relationships, geographical proximity, and shared distrust of American power, even as their children may prefer the American way. Regardless, we must remember that, while we are at war with no democracy, we have had to intervene in a lot of autocracies in the last twenty years. Far better to suffer the chastisements of a democratically elected Saudi parliament for, say, our rejection of [the] Kyoto [greenhouse gas emissions treaty] than to stand by while the Saudi royal family bankrolls the spread of extremism around the world.

Finally, with the Cold War a thing of the past, we must rethink our dealings with caretaker dictators who make noises about moving toward the rule of law, press freedom, and markets but deliver little meaningful reform. The old rationale for bearing with mere authoritarians has crumbled away with the passing of the expansionist Marxist-Leninist totalitarians. Without ever losing sight of our preference for peaceful change, we need to reassess, carefully and thoroughly, the usefulness of propping up strongmen in the name of stability, when to do this is to flout the aspirations of long-suppressed peoples and forget our national principles. Muslims in autocratic Pakistan are dangerous to us, but those in democratic India are not. . . .

Try Freedom

In the Middle East, everything has been tried except freedom. Confronted over the years with Arab Communists, Islamic extremists, and every manner of dictator, American policy-makers have juggled the imperatives of countering Soviet expansionism, fighting terrorism, and protecting world commerce in oil. Through it all, the region has remained beset by abject failure. Yet we need not despair and turn isolationist. We must rather accept that the world itself has changed since the Cold War; and in our own national interest, we must make sure that our policies evolve with it. September 11 thrust before us the infiltration of terrorist sleeper cells into the West, the appeasement of murderous Islamists by Arab dictators, and the terrorism on the West Bank. In the process, we lost the easy option of propping up the status quo—and the Islamic world lost the privilege of being different.

"Even if the United States . . . vigorously pursued political reform in the region, democratic results would be highly unlikely."

The United States Cannot Impose Democracy on the Middle East

Marina Ottaway, Thomas Carothers, Amy Hawthorne, and Daniel Brumberg

In the following viewpoint four scholars criticize the idea that the United States could create an upsurge in Middle East democracy by toppling Iraqi leader Saddam Hussein. They contend that numerous internal obstacles make any quick democratic transformation of that region a fantasy. The United States must balance democracy promotion with other important U.S. interests, including garnering help in the war on terrorism, finding a solution to the Israeli-Palestinian conflict, and maintaining access to oil. Marina Ottaway is the author of several books on comparative politics. Thomas Carothers is the author of *Aiding Democracy Abroad: The Learning Curve*. Amy Hawthorne is a specialist in Arab politics. Daniel Brumberg is a professor of government at Georgetown University.

As you read, consider the following questions:
1. What experiences with democracy promotion in other countries do the authors describe?
2. What three main issues complicate the achievement of democracy in the Middle East, according to the authors?

Marina Ottaway, Thomas Carothers, Amy Hawthorne, and Daniel Brumberg, "Democratic Mirage in the Middle East," *CEIP Policy Brief*, October 2002. Copyright © 2002 by Carnegie Endowment for International Peace. www.ceip. org. Reproduced by permission.

From within the Bush administration and on the editorial pages of America's major newspapers, a growing chorus of voices is expounding an extraordinarily expansive, optimistic view of a new democratizing mission for America in the Middle East. The rhetoric has reached extraordinary heights. We are told that toppling [Iraqi leader] Saddam Hussein would allow the United States to rapidly democratize Iraq and by so doing unleash a democratic tsunami across the Islamic World. Some believe that a pro-democracy campaign in the Middle East could produce a democratic boom comparable in magnitude and significance to the one produced by the end of the Cold War.

It is good that the question of democracy in the Middle East is finally receiving serious attention. Although the United States has, over the years, offered tepid encouragement for political reform in the Arab world and funded some democracy aid programs there, past efforts were timid, erratic, and not reinforced at senior diplomatic levels. For far too long, Washington coasted on the complacent and erroneous assumption that the stability of the autocratic regimes of the Middle East could at least protect U.S. national security. Now the pendulum has swung. U.S. officials no longer see these regimes as bulwarks against Islamic extremists, but consider them responsible for the discontent that fuels terrorism and, in the case of Saudi Arabia, for the financing of extremist groups. But obstacles to democracy in the Middle East are many and go well beyond the autocratic nature of the present regimes to span a host of economic, sociopolitical, and historical factors. These realities do not mean the Middle East will never democratize or that the United States has no role to play. But they do mean that the path will be long, hard, and slow and that American expectations and plans should be calibrated accordingly.

Democratizing Iraq

It is hard not to feel the attraction of the tsunami idea—the tantalizing notion that with one hard blow in Iraq the United States can unleash a tidal wave of democracy in a region long known for resistance to such change. But can it? The United States can certainly oust Saddam Hussein and install a regime that is less repressive domestically and less hostile to U.S. interests. But democracy will not soon be forthcoming.

Experience in other countries where the United States has forcibly removed dictators or helped launch major post-conflict democratic reconstruction indicates a strong need for caution. In Haiti, for example, the 1994 U.S. invasion and the subsequent large-scale reconstruction effort have not led to democracy but instead political chaos, renewed repression, and dismal U.S.-Haiti relations. In post-Dayton Bosnia,[1] the truly massive international reconstruction effort has produced peace and some socioeconomic gains, but only a tenuous political equilibrium that even six years later would collapse if international forces pulled out. . . . It should be noted that all these countries are small, making even forceful intervention manageable. Iraq, with its 23 million inhabitants, would require an intervention on a totally different scale.

The example of Afghanistan[2] is especially sobering. Despite widespread optimism of the initial post-Taliban period and the Bush administration's ringing promises to lead the democratic reconstruction, the political situation in Afghanistan today [in October 2002] is troubled and uncertain. The administration's failure to back up its promises with a genuine commitment to Afghanistan's reconstruction will badly undercut similar promises made about Iraq.

Like Afghanistan, Iraq is a country torn by profound ideological, religious and ethnic conflicts. Before democratization can even begin, the United States would have to assemble a power-sharing agreement among ethnic Kurds, Shiites, and Sunni Muslims. Because no obvious leader is waiting in the wings and the exiled Iraqi opposition is chronically divided, Washington would have to provide the political and, most importantly, military and security infrastructure necessary for holding a new government together. In short, the United States would have to become engaged in nation building on a scale that would dwarf any other such effort

---

1. America and its NATO allies have stationed peacekeeping troops in Bosnia since the 1995 Dayton Accords ended a three-year war in that multiethnic state. 2. The United States military helped Afghan insurgents topple the Taliban regime in late 2001. America subsequently supported the accession of Hamid Karzai as president of Afghanistan in 2002 and continued to station peacekeeping troops in that country.

since the reconstruction of Germany and Japan after World War II. And it would have to stay engaged not just years, but decades, given the depth of change required to make Iraq into a democracy. Thus far the Bush administration has given no indication that it is ready to commit to such a long-term, costly endeavor. All this does not mean that Iraq can never become democratic. But the idea of a quick and easy democratic transformation is a fantasy.

Far-Fetched Notions

Equally doubtful is the idea that a regime change in Iraq would trigger a democratic tsunami in the Middle East. The notion that the fabled "Arab street" would respond to the establishment of a U.S.-installed, nominally democratic Iraqi regime by rising up in a surge of pro-democratic protests, toppling autocracy after autocracy, and installing pro-western, pluralist regimes is far-fetched. No one can predict with any certainty what the precise regional consequences of a U.S. action would be, but they would likely have as many or more negative than positive effects on the near-term potential for democracy.

For example, an invasion would very likely intensify the anti-Americanism already surging around the region, strengthening the hands of hard-line political forces. Autocratic Arab regimes that refused to support the American war effort could benefit from a wave of Arab nationalism and find their position strengthened, at least for a period. Domestic advocates of reform would come under suspicion as unpatriotic. Conversely, by supporting the invasion, several autocratic regimes, including Saudi Arabia and Egypt, might win a reprieve from any new U.S. pressure to democratize.

The formation of a new, more moderate regime in Iraq would unlikely have the inspirational effect some predict. Many Arabs, rather than looking to Iraq as a model, would focus on the fact that Iraq was "liberated" through western intervention, not by a popular Iraqi movement. One powerful current in today's regional discourse emphasizes liberation from excessive western interference in Arab affairs more than liberation from undemocratic leaders.

As to possible ramifications for the future of Palestine,

Ariel Sharon's government in Israel would likely view an American invasion of Iraq as an invitation to skirt the [Palestinian] statehood issue. Unless the Bush administration shows the political will to push now for a two-state solution—a very unlikely scenario given the close links between Israeli hard-liners and administration hawks—victory in Iraq would more likely postpone than advance the creation of a democratic Palestine.

Domino democratization does sometimes occur, as in Latin America and Eastern Europe in the 1980s and 1990s. But while external influences may increase the chance of an initial change in government, what happens next depends on internal conditions. This was certainly the case in the former Soviet Union, where what at first seemed like a wave of democracy petered out in the face of deep-seated domestic obstacles. Today most former Soviet republics are autocracies.

Middle East Realities

Even if the United States ousted Saddam Hussein and vigorously pursued political reform in the region, democratic results would be highly unlikely. Such a policy would certainly shake up the region, but the final outcome in each country would owe much more to domestic factors than to the vigor of U.S. and European reformist zeal. One of the lessons of more than a decade of democracy promotion around the world is that outsiders are usually marginal players. They become the central determinant of political change only if they are willing to intervene massively, impose a de facto protectorate, and stay for an indefinite, long term. No matter what happens in Iraq, such forceful intervention is unthinkable in most Middle East countries.

The Middle East today lacks the domestic conditions that set the stage for democratic change elsewhere. It does not have the previous experience with democracy that facilitated transitions in Central Europe. Even Egypt, which in the early part of the twentieth century had a national bourgeoisie committed to the values of liberal democracy, opted for autocracy fifty years ago. Quite a few countries in the region—Algeria, Egypt, Jordan, and Morocco among them—are liberalized autocracies whose leaders have skillfully used a measure of state-monitored political openness to promote reforms that appear pluralistic but function to preserve autocracy. Through controlled elections, divide-and-rule tactics, state interference in civil society organizations, and the obstruction of meaningful political party systems, these regimes have created deeply entrenched ruling systems that are surprisingly effective at resisting democratic change.

Nor has the Middle East experienced the prolonged periods of economic growth and the resulting dramatic changes in educational standards, living standards, and life styles that led Asian countries like Taiwan and South Korea to democratic change. The picture is instead one of socioeconomic deterioration. Even in the richest oil-producing countries, oil export revenues are no longer sufficient to subsidize rapidly growing populations at previous levels. The population of Saudi Arabia, for example, was less than six million in 1974 at the time of the first oil boom, but it is now sixteen million and growing at one of the highest rates in the world. Through state control of the economy, furthermore, regimes have purchased the support, or at least the quiescence, of key sectors of the citizenry.

Moreover, countries of the Middle East do not benefit from a positive "neighborhood effect," the regional, locally grown pressure to conform that helped democratize Latin America. On the contrary, neighborhood norms in the Middle East encourage repressive, authoritarian regimes.

Three Complicating Factors

Beyond these daunting obstacles, at least three issues complicate the achievement of democracy in the Middle East:

Islamism. The issue is not whether Islam and democracy are incompatible in an absolute sense. Like Christianity and Judaism, Islam is far too complex a religion, with too many schools of thought, for the question even to make sense. Rather, the issue is the existence in all Middle Eastern countries, and indeed in all countries with a substantial Moslem population, of both legal and clandestine political movements that use illiberal interpretations of Islam to mobilize their followers. Since these "Islamist" movements enjoy considerable grassroots support and local authenticity, they are most likely to benefit from democratic openings. Truly free and fair elections in any country of the Middle East would likely assure Islamist parties a substantial share of the vote, or possibly even a majority, as would have happened in Algeria in 1992 had the elections not been cancelled. Democratization ironically raises the possibility of bringing to power political parties that might well abrogate democracy itself. This is a different version of the old Cold War–era fears: communist parties in Western Europe and elsewhere would come to power through elections only to impose rad-

---

The Democracy Dilemma

American policymakers have long grappled with the so-called "democracy dilemma" in the Arab world: How should the United States promote political liberalization without threatening core U.S. interests in the Middle East? These interests include maintaining Israel's security and well-being, ensuring reliable access to petroleum reserves in the Gulf, preventing terrorism and the spread of weapons of mass destruction, and supporting U.S. investment. . . .

Many recognize that the lack of political freedom in the Arab world . . . may endanger U.S. interests in the long term. Repression and exclusion from meaningful political participation sow the seeds of hopelessness, extremism and violent upheaval. And as the connection between economic development and good governance becomes increasingly clear, the U.S. is concerned that the Arab world's sclerotic political systems are inhibiting the region's integration into the global economy.

Yet supporting genuine democratic change may not only provoke tension with Arab regimes whose cooperation is essential to the achievement of U.S. interests, it also risks bringing to power leaders who would actively reject American values. Across the region, free elections might replace current regimes, whether monarchies or secular republics, with some kind of Islamist leadership. The U.S. considers this a worse option since many Islamists reject U.S. influence in the Middle East. Throughout the Arab world, with a choice between a less-than-democratic status quo and the potential outcome of a democratization process—a power transfer to an anti-U.S. Islamist-oriented government—the U.S. has preferred the former.

Amy Hawthorne, *Foreign Service Journal*, February 2001.

ical change. However, continuing to exclude or marginalize Islamist political participation would doom democracy by silencing a voice that resonates with an important segment of the public. Doing so would only provide governments with a justification for maintaining excessive controls over the entire political sphere, thereby stunting the development of other popular forces. Many governments, such as those in Algeria, Jordan, Lebanon, Morocco, Turkey, and Yemen, have tried to skirt this dilemma by giving Islamists a chance to participate in politics while at the same time preventing them from actually assuming political power, but this solution also augurs poorly for democracy.

Conflict with Israel. Resentment against the state of Israel, particularly against the Israeli occupation of the West Bank and Gaza, creates a measure of solidarity between Arab leaders and their citizens that is exploited regularly by autocrats to deflect attention from their own shortcomings. Until there is a two-state solution of the Israeli-Palestinian conflict that gives security and dignity to both parties, resentment will infuse all aspects of Arab politics and obscure the question of democracy.

Perceptions of the United States. There is a widespread perception in the Middle East that the Bush administration is embracing the cause of democracy promotion not out of real commitment, but because doing so provides a convenient justification for American intervention in Iraq and the acceptance of the Israeli reoccupation of the West Bank. Unconditional support of Israel, combined with the Sharon government's publicly stated objective of deferring Palestinian statehood, feeds a widespread feeling that the U.S. government cannot be trusted. America's long support of Arab autocracies adds to this perception, thus undermining its credibility as an advocate of change in the Middle East.

Beyond the Mirage

The United States should promote democracy in the Middle East recognizing that quick change is a mirage. The goals must be initially modest, and the commitment to change long term. . . .

A serious program of long-term support for Middle East

democracy would need to follow these guidelines:

- *Do not reflexively attempt to marginalize Islamist groups.* Differentiate instead between the truly extremist organizations that must be isolated because they are committed to violence and those amenable to working legally to achieve their goals. Develop strategies to encourage political processes in which moderate Islamists, along with other emerging forces, can compete fairly and over time gain incentives to moderate their illiberal ideologies. To do this, the United States needs to acquire a much better understanding of the relevant organizations in each country. It will not be easy and it entails some risk. But the only means of containing dangerous extremist groups without perpetuating wholesale repression is to open the door of legal political activity to the more moderate organizations.

- *Do not overemphasize support for westernized nongovernmental organizations and individuals with impeccable liberal credentials but little influence in their societies.* Democracy promoters need to engage as much as possible in a dialogue with a wide cross section of influential elites: mainstream academics, journalists, moderate Islamists, and members of the professional associations who play a political role in some Arab countries, rather than only the narrow world of westernized democracy and human rights advocates.

- *Don't confuse a "sell America" campaign with democracy promotion.* The U.S. government has launched a major public relations campaign to burnish America's image in the Arab world. Whatever the value of this much-discussed effort, it has little to do with the politically nuanced task of pressuring governments on human rights and institutional reforms, and of supporting key civil groups and the like. Movement toward democracy and movement toward a more positive view of American culture and society are not synonymous.

- *Do not support lackluster institutional reform programs—such as with stagnant parliaments and judiciaries—in lieu of real political reform.* Push the liberalized autocracies of the region, such as in Bahrain, Egypt, Kuwait, Jordan, and Lebanon, beyond the superficial political reforms they use to sustain themselves. This will require pressuring such states to undertake true political restructuring, allow the development of political parties, and open up more space for political contestation.

• *Account for major differences in political starting points and potential for political change. Shape policies accordingly.* Be clear about the goal in each country: regime change, slow liberalization, and democratization are not the same thing. Policies to achieve one goal are not necessarily appropriate for the others. In particular, a sudden regime change would probably make democratization a more remote prospect for many countries because it would too quickly tip the balance in favor of the groups that are best organized and enjoy grassroots support, Islamist organizations in most cases. . . .

America's Limited Leverage

The idea of instant democratic transformation in the Middle East is a mirage. The fact that the Bush administration has suddenly changed its mind about the importance of democracy in the Middle East has not changed the domestic political equation in any country of the region. Furthermore, the United States has limited leverage in most Arab countries. In other regions, the United States, together with Europe and international organizations, often used the lever of economic assistance to force political reform on reluctant governments. But oil-rich countries do not receive aid. Poor countries in the region do, but the United States can hardly afford to use this aid as a weapon for political reform without jeopardizing other interests. The United States already wants a lot from Arab states. It wants help in the war on terrorism. It wants their oil. It wants cooperation in finding a solution to the Israeli-Palestinian conflict. It wants access to military installations to wage war on Iraq. It cannot afford to antagonize the very regimes whose cooperation it seeks. The United States will be forced to work with existing regimes toward gradual reform—and this is a good thing. If a tidal wave of political change actually came to pass, the United States would not be even remotely prepared to cope with the resulting instability and need for large-scale building of new political systems.

"U.S. dependency on Middle East oil can be greatly reduced, if not eliminated, through domestic energy conservation."

The United States Should Reduce Its Dependency on Middle East Oil

Part I: *Ellsworth American*; Part II: *Christian Century*

The United States imports more than half the oil it consumes, 20 percent of which comes from the Middle East. In the following two-part viewpoint, the editors of the *Ellsworth American* and the *Christian Century* argue that because of America's economic dependence on imported oil, the country has been compelled to support corrupt regimes, and has been hampered in its ability to support peace in the region. The authors call for serious measures to reduce oil consumption, such as higher gasoline taxes and stricter fuel-efficiency regulations for automobiles and sport utility vehicles (SUVs). The *Ellsworth American* is a weekly newspaper based in Maine. The *Christian Century* is a national liberal Christian publication.

As you read, consider the following questions:

1. How much of the world's oil reserves lie within the Middle East, according to the editors?
2. What possible scenarios do the editors of the *Ellsworth American* describe concerning Saudi Arabia?
3. What specific recommendations on energy conservation do the editors of the *Christian Century* make?

I

Well over half of all the proven oil reserves in the world sit beneath the sands of one of the most volatile and unpredictable regions of the world—the area surrounding the Persian Gulf. The developed and developing nations of the world, and most particularly the United States, rely almost totally on oil for transport and a multitude of other uses. Without it, our planes would not fly, our cars, trucks, buses and trains would not run, even our ships would not sail. The generation of electricity would be sharply curtailed, millions of homes would be left without heat, and our manufacturing industries would collapse. Our economy, and others, would grind to a halt.

Some will say that we need not worry since oil-exporting nations, such as Saudi Arabia, which by itself sits on a fourth of all proven oil reserves, and the buyers of its oil are mutually dependent. One needs a supply, the other a market. While the current Saudi regime is regarded as an ally of the United States, its stability is far from assured. Recent history illustrates that there are fundamentalist revolutionaries such as the Taliban within the Islamic world who would willingly consign their subjects to abject poverty to bring the West to its knees. The Middle East is a breeding ground for terrorists of the sort who launched the September 11 [2001, terrorist] attacks on America. The possibility that nuclear weapons already may be in the hands of those terrorists or the governments who overtly or covertly support them is a risk that can be ignored only at our own peril. Several Middle East countries, including Saudi Arabia, are vulnerable to those revolutionaries. Once in power, they easily could cause short-term or long-term disruptions in the supply of oil, either by sharply increasing prices, shutting off exports or even destroying the oil fields.

America's Oil Addiction

In the face of such huge risk, neither our national leaders nor our citizens seem willing to make the choices—choices that would be far less painful than those wrought by any major disruption in oil supplies—that are needed to reduce, even modestly, America's addiction to oil.

Given current and projected consumption levels over the next few decades, dependence on Middle East oil will increase, not decrease. Many of the big fields outside the embrace of OPEC [Organization of Petroleum Exporting Countries] are entering a period of decline or nearing depletion. The cost of finding and developing other non-OPEC reserves is huge, and growing.

What United States citizens and their government must do is to embrace every conceivable conservation measure for the short term and implement energy efficiency for the long term. At this point, neither is happening in any meaningful way.

Studies suggest that America could reduce fuel use on the highways by as much as 20 percent with technologies already available. But the partisan Congress has no willingness to challenge automobile companies and the American public, either by mandating significant increases in fuel economy laws or by boosting taxes on gasoline and other petroleum fuels. Government investment and support for developing alternative energy sources is minimal at best.

The President's [George W. Bush] answer to the problem is to tap oil reserves beneath the Arctic National Wildlife Refuge in Alaska, but its effect on our consumption of imported oil would be nearly negligible.

Leaders within Congress and the Bush administration doubtless recognize the national security implications posed by our dependence on OPEC and Middle East oil. Now they must somehow find the will to do something about it—before time runs out.

II

The U.S.'s approach to the Middle East frequently seems less policy than fated inevitability. The U.S. requires oil from that region for its survival, therefore it underwrites despotic and corrupt regimes, and bears the consequences of those alliances. Yet neither the need nor the alliances are written in the stars.

Energy Conservation

U.S. dependency on Middle East oil can be greatly reduced, if not eliminated, through domestic energy conservation.

More specifically, the U.S.'s need for Middle East oil would plummet if Americans chose to reduce their consumption of gasoline. Writing in *Foreign Affairs* (hardly an organ of the Green movement), Amory and Hunter Lovins have claimed that if Americans "had simply bought new cars that got 5 mpg more than they did, [the U.S.] would no longer have needed Persian Gulf oil."

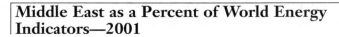

Middle East as a Percent of World Energy Indicators—2001

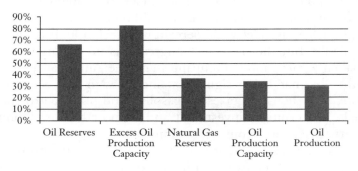

Energy Information Administration

Energy efficiency has increased in many sectors of American industry and domestic life—from home heating and cooling systems to innovative light bulbs. But fuel economy for vehicles has actually dropped from 26.2 mpg in the 1980s to a current average of 24.7 mpg. Raising federal taxes on gasoline and requiring vehicles to meet higher fuel-efficiency standards would help reverse this trend.

Americans pay some of the lowest gasoline taxes in the Western world. A little over a quarter of the price of gasoline at the pump goes to federal, state and local taxes. In Canada that figure is around 42 percent, and in Europe taxes can account for more than 75 percent of the price paid at the pump. Although gas prices over $2.00 a gallon are front-page news in the U.S., Europeans have been paying between $3.00 and $5.00 per gallon for years.

Increasing the federal tax on gasoline would help pay for big budget items that will continue to emerge from the

September 11 crisis and the war on terrorism, and would act as an incentive for Americans to drive less or purchase more energy efficient vehicles, or both.

However, in a country with poor public transportation, in which many workers must drive considerable distances to work, an increased federal gas tax would disproportionately affect lower-income households. For this reason, a bump up in gas taxes must be modest. Greater emphasis must be placed on achieving increased fuel efficiency for the vehicles Americans drive.

Fuel Efficiency Standards Must Be Raised

Closing the SUV loophole would be a step in the right direction. Starting in 1975, when fuel-efficiency standards were being set for vehicles, light trucks used primarily in agriculture and construction were granted lower targets than automobiles. Those targets now are 27.5 mpg for autos and 20.7 mpg for light trucks. Since 1975, however, the category "light truck" has come to include gas guzzling SUVs and vans that now account for more than half of all new car sales in the U.S. (Currently the average mileage for SUVs, vans and pickups is 18 mpg.) A standard tailored for working trucks now applies to vehicles that haul mainly groceries and soccer balls. Bringing this class of vehicles up to the same standard of efficiency as the one that currently exists for autos (not an unreasonable goal) could save as much as 1 million barrels of oil per day.

High-efficiency hybrid gas-electric cars like the Toyota Prius (49 mpg) and Honda's Insight (67 mpg) offer alternatives to the behemoths cruising America's highways. So does the development of light rail systems linking regional urban areas. These and other options for increased energy conservation would benefit the environment that sustains us all, and would free the U.S. from its dependency on Middle East oil. Released from that dependency, the U.S. may become a truly independent and honest broker of general peace in the region.

Americans displayed an immediate willingness to sacrifice their blood to aid fellow citizens following the September 11 attacks. It's time to sacrifice, for the common good, the profligate use of another viscous liquid.

"Politically correct, misguided energy schemes will not make America more independent."

Calls to Reduce America's Dependency on Middle East Oil Are Unrealistic

Henry Payne and Diane Katz

Henry Payne is an editorial cartoonist and writer for the *Detroit News*. Diane Katz is an editorial writer for the *Detroit News*. In the following viewpoint they respond to the argument that America must reduce oil and gasoline consumption to reduce its dependency on Middle East oil. Oil is produced throughout the world, Katz and Payne write, nullifying the ability of Middle East nations to manipulate global supplies. In addition, the authors criticize conservation programs such as mandated fuel-efficiency standards in automobiles, as well as proposals to develop hydrogen-powered cars, arguing that these actions are costly and will not achieve the goal of reducing economic dependence on the Middle East.

As you read, consider the following questions:

1. What has happened to oil prices since September 11, 2001, according to Katz and Payne?
2. What would raising automobile fuel-efficiency standards accomplish, according to the authors?
3. What problems exist with replacing gasoline with hydrogen fuel cells, according to Katz and Payne?

Any crisis in the Middle East inevitably prompts Washington to scapegoat the automobile as a threat to national security. The dust had barely settled on lower Manhattan last fall [following the September 11, 2001, terrorist attacks] before calls went forth—from pundits and pols across the spectrum—to relinquish our "gas-guzzlers" in the name of energy independence.

But just as the Cassandras will dominate media coverage of energy, so will Middle Eastern oil continue to fuel America's vehicles for the foreseeable future. Simple economics, geography, and consumer choice all demand it.

A Dangerous Addiction?

Since Sept. 11, Washington has mobilized to end our "dangerous addiction" to foreign energy sources. Senators John Kerry and John McCain are proposing dramatic increases in federal fuel-economy standards. The . . . Natural Resources Defense Council is insisting that we could cut gasoline consumption by 50 percent over ten years—if only the feds would mandate what and where we drove.

Even the "oil men" in the Bush administration have advocated doling out millions in research subsidies for hydrogen fuel cells that supposedly would replace the internal-combustion engine. The project, Energy Secretary Spencer Abraham announced in January [2002], is "rooted in President [George W.] Bush's call to reduce American reliance on foreign oil."

In fact, the price of oil has declined since Sept. 11, as it consistently has for decades, and with producers scattered all over the world, no single nation or region can stop the flow.

But supporters of a comprehensive energy policy seem undeterred by these realities. "Logic," [columnist] Robert Samuelson writes in the *Washington Post*, "is no defense against instability. We need to make it harder for [Middle Easterners] to use the oil weapon and take steps to protect ourselves if it is used. Even if we avoid trouble now, the threat will remain."

Past efforts to attain a petroleum-free utopia, however, have largely failed. For example, despite three decades of federal fuel-economy standards, oil imports as a share of

U.S. consumption have risen from 35 to 59 percent.

A market-based solution, such as a gas tax, is the most obvious approach to cutting consumption, but even environmentalists concede that proposing one would spell political suicide. Moreover, gas taxes are an expensive solution and come with no guarantee of energy independence. The European Union, for example, taxes gas up to $4 per gallon—and still imports over half its oil.

So instead of enraging consumers at the pump, Washington has largely relied on backdoor taxes.

Fuel-Economy Standards

The regulatory regime known as CAFE (Corporate Average Fuel Economy) was hatched in the wake of the oil-price shocks of the early 1970s, when sedans still made up most of the nation's fleet. Instead of the redesigned smaller, lighter, and less powerful vehicles, however, consumers flocked to minivans, small trucks, and sport utility vehicles, which are held to a lower CAFE standard (20.7 mpg versus the 27.5 mpg required for cars).

Today, both passenger cars and light trucks are more efficient than ever, having improved 114 percent and 56 percent, respectively, since 1974. But gasoline is so cheap, despite continuing Middle Eastern crises, that on average Americans are driving twice as many miles as in years past.

A . . . study by H. Sterling Burnett of the National Center for Policy Analysis found that raising CAFE standards by 40 percent—as Kerry and others recommend—would not "reduce future U.S. dependence on foreign oil." CAFE's only function is to keep regulators busy calculating elaborate formulas for determining compliance in which manufacturers then look for loopholes. (CAFE requires that a manufacturer's trucks meet an average standard of 20.7 mpg. Thus DaimlerChrysler AG, for example, designates its popular PT Cruiser as a "truck" in order to offset the low mpg of its large SUVs, such as the Dodge Durango.)

Worse, stricter CAFE standards would surely undermine the very economic security that proponents vow to protect. The profits of U.S. automakers—and tens of thousands of UAW [United Auto Workers] jobs—depend on sales of

SUVs and light trucks. According to an analysis by Andrew N. Kleit, a professor at Pennsylvania State University, the Kerry CAFE proposal would reduce the profits of General Motors by $3.8 billion, of Ford by $3.4 billion, and of Daimler-Chrysler by $2 billion. Foreign manufacturers, which largely specialize in smaller vehicles, would see a profit increase of $4.4 billion.

Limits of Hydrogen

Evidently hoping to shield automakers from a CAFE assault—and to win PR points for expanded domestic drilling—the Bush administration has embraced the latest alternative-fuel fad: the hydrogen fuel cell.

The Bush plan replaces the Partnership for a New Generation of Vehicles, [former vice president] Al Gore's vain attempt to produce an affordable, emissions-free family sedan capable of 80 mpg by 2004. Over eight years, Washington pumped more than $1.5 billion into the program—in addition to the $1.5 billion sunk into it by the Big Three. In its annual review of the project last August [2001], the National Research Council judged the super-car goals to be inherently "unrealistic."

The Bush plan has drawn broad political support. Former Clinton chief of staff John Podesta cheers, "The next step is hydrogen-powered fuel-cell vehicles. But the only way to get these vehicles out of the lab and onto the road is with incentives and requirements aimed at producing 100,000 vehicles by 2010, 2.5 million by 2020."

But the 100-year dominance of conventional internal-combustion engines over alternatives is no accident. A quick primer on the complexities of hydrogen power helps explain why.

Hydrogen's status as the new darling of the sustainable-energy movement is understandable. Its promise lies first in its performance: Unlike ethanol, it supplies more energy per pound than gasoline. When used to power an automobile, its only emission is water—making it especially attractive to an industry already under pressure from clean-air and global-warming rules. And hydrogen is one of the most plentiful elements on the planet.

The trouble is, hydrogen always comes married to another element—as in methane gas or water.

Most fuel-cell technology today relies on hydrogen extracted from methane, in a process that emits large quantities of greenhouse gases. And as *Car and Driver* magazine's technical analyst, Patrick Bedard, explains, domestic sources of methane are "[t]oo limited to serve any significant demand for automobiles." A study by the Argonne National Laboratory concluded that the U.S. would have to look to foreign sources—primarily in Russia and Iran, and in other Middle East nations.

Goodbye, oil dependence. Hello, methane dependence.

No Oil Crisis

The global view suggests, in fact, that there is no supply crisis. We know there's a lot more oil worldwide now than in the 1970s. Using increasingly advanced probes and sensors, surveys that once estimated total global reserves at 650 billion now find more than a trillion barrels. . . .

Buying oil is much easier today, too. Then and now, the Middle East oil cartel sat on roughly two thirds of known reserves, but in 1970 its members sold directly to customers—and could punish them individually. Today oil is sold on an international market mediated by thousands of middlemen and futures exchanges around the world, a system that has done much to undermine OPEC's [Organization of Petroleum Exporting Countries] clout. "They can't cut off our oil supply, they can only cut off oil supply," says Professor William Hogan of Harvard. "It's a very blunt political weapon, so they stopped using it as a weapon."

Tony Emerson et al., *Newsweek*, April 8, 2002.

Given these hurdles, attention is turning instead to electrolysis—the extraction of hydrogen from water, which is readily obtainable along America's ample coasts. Electrolysis is, however, the most energy-intensive process of any fuel alternative; studies differ on whether it would consume more carbon-based fuels than the use of hydrogen would save. What is certain, points out Stanford University professor John McCarthy, is that "the advantage of hydrogen, if you have to burn carbon fuels (coal, oil, or gas) to manufacture it, would be negligible."

In other words, McCarthy explains, the unspoken truth about hydrogen is that "it is a synonym for nuclear power.". . . .

Ironically, many of the political voices now embracing hydrogen fuel are the same ones that have prevented the construction of a single new U.S. nuclear plant in 25 years. . . .

Gasoline Remains the Answer

For now, the answer is still gasoline. Compared with the technical barriers to developing alternative fuels, there already exist numerous market mechanisms to mitigate potential oil shortages. As suggested by Donald Losman, a National Defense University economist, these include: stockpiling, futures contracts, diversifying the supplier base, and relaxing the restrictions that currently mandate some 13 different fuel blends in 30 cities.

Dramatic improvements in fuel efficiency also could be achieved if Washington allowed automakers to market diesel-powered vehicles. In Germany, for example, Volkswagen mass markets the 80-mpg Lupo, which is powered by a direct-injection diesel engine. But that's anathema to American greens who insist—without evidence—that diesel's particulate emissions are dangerous to public health. All fuels require trade-offs, of course. But politically correct, misguided energy schemes will not make America more independent. Gasoline remains by far the best deal we have.

Periodical Bibliography

The following articles have been selected to supplement the diverse views presented in this chapter.

Gawdat Bahgat	"Oil and Militant Islam: Strains on U.S.-Saudi Relations," *World Affairs*, Winter 2003.
Michael Barone	"Remaking the Middle East," *U.S. News & World Report*, December 2, 2002.
Joseph A. Cari Jr.	"From the Center (Proposed Marshall Plan for the Middle East)," *Wilson Quarterly*, Spring 2002.
Robert Dreyfuss	"The Thirty Year Itch," *Mother Jones*, March/April 2003.
Economist	"A Delicate Balance; America and the Arab World," May 4, 2002.
Economist	"Zigzagging; America and the Conflict," April 6, 2002.
Frank J. Gaffney Jr.	"U.S. Would Sell Out Israel by Pushing for Land-for-Peace Deal," *Insight on the News*, April 15, 2002.
Adam Garfinkle	"The Impossible Imperative? Conjuring Arab Democracy," *The National Interest*, Fall 2002.
Reuel Marc Gerecht	"Appeasing Arab Dictators," *Weekly Standard*, April 8, 2002.
Christopher Hitchens	"Single Standards," *Nation*, May 13, 2002.
Lawrence F. Kaplan	"Neutrality Act—The Limits of American Influence," *New Republic*, April 15, 2002.
Alfred M. Lilienthal	"The Israel Quagmire (Thoughts for the U.S. Citizen)," *Vital Speeches*, December 15, 2001.
Johanna McGeary	"Looking Beyond Saddam," *Time*, March 3, 2003.
Michael B. Oren	"Does the United States Finally Understand Israel?" *Commentary*, July/August 2002.
David Pryce-Jones	"Oslo and Other Illusions," *National Review*, December 9, 2002.
Michael Renner	"Oil & Blood," *World Watch*, January/February 2003.
Jerry Taylor	"Oh No! That '70s Show: Against Carterism in Energy Policy," *National Review*, March 25, 2002.

Kenneth T. Walsh et al.	"Time to Step In," *U.S. News & World Report*, April 15, 2002.
Wilson Quarterly	"Debating Preemptive War," Winter 2003.
Fareed Zakaria	"How to Save the Arab World," *Newsweek*, December 24, 2001.
Stephen Zunes	"Problems with Current U.S. Policy," *Foreign Policy in Focus*, May 20, 2002.

CHAPTER 4

Is Peace Between Israel and the Palestinians Possible?

Chapter Preface

For much of the 1990s, what became known as the "Oslo process" created a sense of optimism for many that peace between Israel and the Palestinians was indeed possible. Such optimism has been replaced in the new millennium by disillusionment as peace negotiations have stalled and Israel has been racked with renewed violence and terrorist attacks.

The Oslo process began in February 1993, when representatives from Israel and the Palestine Liberation Organization (PLO) participated in secret talks in Oslo, Norway. These talks focused on implementing eventual Palestinian self-rule by withdrawing Israeli troops from the Gaza Strip and the town of Jericho (areas occupied by Israel following the 1967 Six-Day War). A newly created Palestinian Authority (PA), led by Yasser (Yasir) Arafat, was to govern these areas. The Palestine Liberation Organization in turn was to renounce its previous goal of destroying the Jewish state of Israel. In September 1993 Arafat and Israeli prime minister Yitzhak Rabin met in Washington, D.C., to sign this historic Oslo agreement. This agreement was supplemented by the Oslo II accords, signed in September 1995, and the 1998 Wye River Memorandum, both of which gave more Israeli-occupied West Bank territory over to full or limited Palestinian rule and reaffirmed PA commitments against terrorist activity against Israel. These agreements, as well as a separate 1994 peace treaty between Israel and Jordan, increased hopes for peace in the Middle East.

The Oslo process has been continually beset with problems that threaten to derail it, however. In 1994 violence broke out in the West Bank and Gaza as Jewish settlers resisted the government's efforts to hand territory over to the Palestinians. In November 1995 Rabin was assassinated by an Orthodox Jew unhappy with the Oslo accords. Palestinian militants, some of whom opposed the Palestinian Authority's recognition of Israel, committed terrorist attacks, including some suicide bombings, against Israel, although such terrorist attacks diminished somewhat after the 1998 Wye agreement.

In the summer of 2000, American president Bill Clinton

attempted to bring Arafat and Israeli prime minister Ehud Barak together to hammer out a final peace agreement, but negotiations failed to bridge differences over several key issues, including control of Jerusalem and the right of Palestinian refugees to return to Israel. In September 2000, with peace negotiations at an impasse, a new wave of violence swept through Israel after Palestinians protested a visit by Israeli political leader Ariel Sharon to a Jerusalem site holy to both Jews and Muslims. After Sharon was elected prime minister in February 2001, Israel escalated its military actions against suspected Palestinian terrorists. Israel has reoccupied much of the territory that it had handed over to the Palestinian Authority in previous years and has engaged in aggressive police and military action against suspected terrorists. Palestinian militants have committed numerous acts of terrorism against Israelis, such as the suicide bombing of a bus in Haifa on March 5, 2003, that left fifteen dead. Between September 2000 and February 2003, approximately nineteen hundred Palestinians and seven hundred Israelis perished in either terrorist or military actions.

The violence that has occurred in the years following the signing of the Oslo agreement has caused many to conclude that the Oslo process has reached a dead end. The viewpoints in this chapter examine what prospects remain for peace between Israelis and Palestinians. The enduring hostilities between the two, as evidenced by the breakdown of the Oslo peace process, certainly makes optimism difficult to maintain.

1

"Palestinians are ready to end the conflict. We are ready to sit down now with any Israeli leader."

A Negotiated Peace Between Israel and the Palestinians Is Possible

Yasir Arafat

Yasir (Yasser) Arafat was elected president of the Palestinian Authority in 1996. Prior to that he had already come to personify Palestinian resistance to Israel as chairman of the Palestine Liberation Organization, which he has led since 1964. The following viewpoint was published in 2002 when he was under heavy criticism for failing to curtail Palestinian terrorist attacks against Israelis. In it, Arafat condemns terrorism and sets forth his vision of Middle East peace, which he states must include the creation of a sovereign Palestinian state out of territory occupied by Israel since the 1967 war, and the sharing of Jerusalem as the capital of two states, Palestine and Israel. He argues that the Palestinians remain willing to negotiate with Israeli leaders to achieve such a peace.

As you read, consider the following questions:

1. What step did the Palestine National Council take in 1988, according to Arafat?
2. What does Arafat list as the main demands of the Palestinians?
3. What criticism does Arafat make of Israeli prime minister Ariel Sharon?

Yasir Arafat, "The Palestinian Vision of Peace," *The New York Times*, February 3, 2002. Copyright © 2002 by The New York Times Company. Reproduced by permission.

For the past 16 months [since 2000], Israelis and Palestinians have been locked in a catastrophic cycle of violence, a cycle which only promises more bloodshed and fear. The cycle has led many to conclude that peace is impossible, a myth borne out of the ignorance of the Palestinian position. Now is the time for the Palestinians to state clearly, and for the world to hear clearly, the Palestinian vision.

But first, let me be very clear. I condemn the attacks carried out by terrorist groups against Israeli civilians. These groups do not represent the Palestinian people or their legitimate aspirations for freedom. They are terrorist organizations and I am determined to put an end to their activities.

The Palestinian Vision

The Palestinian vision of peace is an independent and viable Palestinian state on the territories occupied by Israel in 1967, living as an equal neighbor alongside Israel with peace and security for both the Israeli and Palestinian peoples. In 1988, the Palestine National Council adopted a historic resolution calling for the implementation of applicable United Nations resolutions, particularly, Resolutions 242 and 338.[1] The Palestinians recognized Israel's right to exist on 78 percent of historic Palestine[2] with the understanding that we would be allowed to live in freedom on the remaining 22 percent under Israeli occupation since 1967. Our commitment to that two state solution remains unchanged, but unfortunately, also remains unreciprocated.

We seek true independence and full sovereignty: The right to control our own airspace, water resources and borders; the right to develop our own economy, to have normal commercial relations with our neighbors, and to travel freely. In short, we seek only what the free world now enjoys and only what Israel insists on for itself: the right to control our own destiny and to take our place among free nations.

1. Resolution 242, passed in 1967, called for Israel to return land seized in the 1967 war and for the nations to respect each other's right to exist within secure boundaries. Resolution 338, passed in 1973, called for a cease-fire of the Yom Kippur War and implementation of Resolution 242.   2. The territory of "historic Palestine" refers to that held by Great Britain under a League of Nations mandate from 1920 to 1948, and which was partitioned by the United Nations into Jewish and Arab states in 1947.

In addition, we seek a fair and just solution to the plight of Palestinian refugees who for 54 years have not been permitted to return to their homes.[3] We understand Israel's demographic concerns and understand that the right of return of Palestinian refugees, a right guaranteed under international law and United Nations Resolution 194, must be implemented in a way that takes into account such concerns. However, just as we Palestinians must be realistic with respect to Israel's demographic desires, Israelis too must be realistic in understanding that there can be no solution to the Israeli-Palestinian conflict if the legitimate rights of these innocent civilians continue to be ignored. Left unresolved, the refugee issue has the potential to undermine any permanent peace agreement between Palestinians and Israelis. How is a Palestinian refugee to understand that his or her right of return will not be honored but those of Kosovar Albanians, Afghans and East Timorese have been?

A Reconciliation Between Peoples

There are those who claim that I am not a partner in peace. In response, I say Israel's peace partner is, and always has been, the Palestinian people. Peace is not a signed agreement between individuals—it is reconciliation between peoples. Two peoples cannot reconcile when one demands control over the other, when one refuses to treat the other as a partner in peace, when one uses the logic of power rather than the power of logic. Israel has yet to understand that it cannot have peace while denying justice. As long as the occupation of Palestinian lands continues, as long as Palestinians are denied freedom, then the path to the "peace of the brave" that I embarked upon with my late partner Yitzhak Rabin,[4] will be littered with obstacles.

The Palestinian people have been denied their freedom for far too long and are the only people in the world still living under foreign occupation. How is it possible that the entire

3. During the 1948 war in which Arab states attacked Israel, only to have Israel successfully defend itself and occupy more land than originally assigned by the United Nations, more than one-half million Palestinians became refugees. 4. Israeli prime minister Yitzhak Rabin, who shared a Nobel Peace Prize with Arafat after the two signed the Oslo peace accords, was assassinated by an Israeli extremist in 1995.

world can tolerate this oppression, discrimination and humiliation? The 1993 Oslo Accord, signed on the White House lawn, promised the Palestinians freedom by May 1999.

Breen. © 2002 by Copley News Service. Reproduced by permission.

Instead, since 1993, the Palestinian people endured a doubling of Israeli settlers, expansion of illegal Israeli settlements on Palestinian land and increased restrictions on freedom of movement. How do I convince my people that Israel is serious about peace while over the past decade, Israel intensified the colonization of Palestinian land from which it was ostensibly negotiating a withdrawal?

Condemning Terrorism

But no degree of oppression and no level of desperation can ever justify the killing of innocent civilians. I condemn terrorism. I condemn the killing of innocent civilians, whether they are Israeli, American or Palestinian, whether they are killed by Palestinian extremists, Israeli settlers, or by the Israeli government. But condemnations do not stop terrorism. To stop terrorism, we must understand that terrorism is simply the symptom, not the disease.

The personal attacks on me currently in vogue may be highly effective in giving Israelis an excuse to ignore their own role in creating the current situation. But these attacks do little to move the peace process forward and, in fact, are not designed to. Many believe that Ariel Sharon, Israel's prime minister, given his opposition to every peace treaty Israel has ever signed, is fanning the flames of unrest in an effort to delay indefinitely a return to negotiations. Regrettably, he has done little to prove them wrong. Israeli government practices of settlement construction, home demolitions, political assassinations, closures and shameful silence in the face of Israeli settler violence and other daily humiliations are clearly not aimed at calming the situation.

The Palestinians have a vision of peace: it is a peace based on the complete end of the occupation and a return to Israel's 1967 borders, the sharing of all Jerusalem as one open city and as the capital of two states, Palestine and Israel. It is a warm peace between two equals enjoying mutually beneficial economic and social cooperation. Despite the brutal repression of Palestinians over the last four decades, I believe when Israel sees Palestinians as equals, and not as a subjugated people upon whom it can impose its will, such a vision can come true. Indeed it must.

Ready to Negotiate

Palestinians are ready to end the conflict. We are ready to sit down now with any Israeli leader, regardless of his history, to negotiate freedom for the Palestinians, a complete end of the occupation, security for Israel and creative solutions to the plight of the refugees while respecting Israel's demographic concerns. But we will only sit down as equals, not as supplicants; as partners, not as subjects; as seekers of a just and peaceful solution, not as a defeated nation grateful for whatever scraps are thrown our way. For despite Israel's overwhelming military advantage, we possess something even greater: the power of justice.

"All attempts to negotiate an end to the Arab-Israeli conflict have merely illustrated the destructive consequences of sacrificing justice to diplomacy."

Peace Negotiations Between Israel and the Palestinians Are Worthless

Robert Tracinski

Robert Tracinski argues that peace negotiations between Israel and the Palestinians are futile because the Palestinian people and Arab nations want nothing less than to destroy Israel. Past efforts at negotiations ended in failure after Palestinian promises to renounce violence and terrorism were not fulfilled, he argues, and there is no reason to believe future diplomatic efforts will succeed. He concludes that the only way to achieve lasting peace is to destroy terrorists, not negotiate with them. Tracinski is the editorial director of the Ayn Rand Institute in Irvine, California.

As you read, consider the following questions:
1. How is President Bush's "road map" similar to past Middle East peace plans, in Tracinski's view?
2. What criticism does the author make of Palestinian leader Mahmoud Abbas?
3. What is the ultimate goal of the Palestinians, according to Tracinski?

Robert Tracinski, "The Road Map to Hell," www.aynrand.org, June 2, 2003.

D espite the big smiles, strong handshakes and profuse waving to the cameras by President [George W.] Bush, [Israeli leader] Ariel Sharon and [Palestinian leader] Mahmoud Abbas in Jordan this week [June 4, 2003], the "road map"[1] to a resolution of the Arab-Israeli conflict is doomed to failure. Why? For the same reason that every Middle East peace plan of the past has failed—because there is no "road map" for achieving peace by negotiating with terrorists.

The new plan consists, as usual, of a sequence of substantive concessions by the victim of terrorism. Israel is to withdraw its military cordon around the staging areas of Palestinian terrorism, relinquish lands crucial to its defense, and recognize a provisional state run by the same old gang of killers. In return, the Palestinians are only required to "declare" an end to violence and take "visible efforts"—whatever that means—to restrain terrorists.

This is not a trade of concessions from which both sides benefit. It is a unilateral surrender to extortion.

In fact, Bush's "road map" is just a retread of previous peace plans. A decade ago, under the Oslo accords,[2] the Palestinians pledged to renounce violence and recognize Israel's right to exist. Then, too, land was to be "traded" for peace—but the Palestinian attacks only escalated. Yet the provisions of the "new" road map are essentially identical to those of the disastrous Oslo deal. Why does anyone expect a different outcome now?

Questioning Palestine's Leadership

Negotiating with terrorists is supposed to work, this time, because of a mere change in personnel. President Bush made his road map conditional on the appointment—by arch-terrorist Yasser Arafat—of a Palestinian leader "not compromised by terror." Thus, Arafat appointed a longtime deputy, Mahmoud Abbas, as the Palestinian Authority's new public face. But Abbas is far from "uncompromised." He is a long-time leader in

---

1. The "road map," formulated by the United States, Europe, Russia, and the United Nations, was presented to Israeli and Palestinian leaders in April 2003. It outlines steps for the creation of a Palestinian state existing next to Israel in the West Bank and Gaza Strip. 2. A series of peace negotiations and agreements made in the 1990s that collapsed in 2000.

Arafat's PLO [Palestine Liberation Organization], and his vaunted opposition to terrorism consists of such statements as: "We are not saying to stop the intifada"—the violent Palestinian uprising—but that "it should be directed."

Israel's Prime Minister Says Terrorism Must First Cease

Israel must defeat terrorism; it cannot negotiate under fire. Israel has made painful concessions for peace before and will demonstrate diplomatic flexibility to make peace again, but it requires first and foremost a reliable partner for peace. In 1977, when Egyptian President Anwar el-Sadat came to Jerusalem, he told the people of Israel, "No more wars." From that point onward, the threat of violence was removed from the Egyptian-Israeli relationship as both negotiated their 1979 Treaty of Peace. King Hussein of Jordan followed the same pattern in 1994. This elementary commitment to permanently renouncing violence in the resolution of political differences has unfortunately not been kept by the present Palestinian leadership.

Ariel Sharon, *New York Times*, June 9, 2002.

The only thing that is supposed to make Abbas a "partner for peace" is that he isn't personally responsible for killing anyone. But if [famed organized crime leader] Al Capone's accountant were appointed as the new negotiator for the mob, would he be a leader "not compromised by crime"? Of course not—and for the same reason, Abbas is just another front man for the Palestinian terrorist establishment. . . .

The Futility of Negotiating with Terrorists

There is a reason we keep getting the same failed peace plan, with the same results. Nothing else is possible, once we accept the vicious policy of negotiating with terrorists.

Legitimate diplomacy can only take place between those who are open to settling their differences through persuasion and who recognize each other's right to live. Yet for decades the Palestinians have consistently adopted brute force and mass murder as their primary means of pursuing their "diplomatic" goals. And their ultimate goal has never changed: they seek the destruction of Israel.

All attempts to negotiate an end to the Arab-Israeli conflict have merely illustrated the destructive consequences of sacrificing justice to diplomacy. Justice demands that one judge rationally the character and conduct of those one deals with, rewarding the good and punishing the evil. To insist on diplomacy as an unqualified virtue—regardless of the nature and conduct of one's foe—does not save lives or resolve conflicts; it merely rewards and emboldens the aggressors. Why should they end terrorism, when it proves, time and time again, to be an effective means of extorting concessions?

This is why it would have been absurd for America to negotiate with [the terrorist group] al Qaeda, the Taliban [Afghanistan's ruling regime that sponsored al Qaeda], or [Iraqi leader] Saddam Hussein. It is also why America should not pressure Israel, our loyal ally in a treacherous region, to negotiate with its terrorist enemies.

One Road to Peace

Peace requires, not the accommodation of the terrorists' demands, but the total and ruthless elimination of the terrorists and those who support them. We should be pressuring Israel, not to surrender to terrorism, but to continue the war on terrorism—to continue it throughout Gaza and the West Bank, and to take it to the planners and suppliers of terrorism in Lebanon and Syria.

This is the only road to peace: to abandon diplomacy and destroy the terrorists.

"Peace requires a new and different Palestinian leadership, so that a Palestinian state can be born."

A New Palestinian Leadership Is a Necessary Precondition for Peace

George W. Bush

George W. Bush, who was inaugurated as America's president in 2001, is the first sitting U.S. president to publicly endorse the idea of creating an independent Palestinian state. In a June 24, 2002 address, excerpted here, Bush describes his vision of a peaceful resolution to the Israeli-Palestinian conflict. Arguing that both Palestinian terrorism and Israeli occupation are untenable, Bush contends that an end to conflict—which would include the creation of a provisional Palestinian state—depends on the selection of new leaders for the Palestinians. Existing leadership in the Palestinian Authority (created in the 1990s to administer parts of the West Bank and Gaza) has failed to contain and eradicate terrorism, Bush contends, and must be replaced. Bush also challenges Israel to take actions to achieve a stable and peaceful Palestinian state.

As you read, consider the following questions:

1. What complaints does Bush make about existing Palestinian political and economic institutions?
2. What rewards does Bush promise the Palestinians if they enact reforms?
3. What steps does Bush say Israel must take to support the creation of a Palestinian state?

George W. Bush, speech, Washington, DC, June 24, 2002.

For too long, the citizens of the Middle East have lived in the midst of death and fear. The hatred of a few holds the hopes of many hostage. The forces of extremism and terror are attempting to kill progress and peace by killing the innocent. And this casts a dark shadow over an entire region. For the sake of all humanity, things must change in the Middle East.

It is untenable for Israeli citizens to live in terror. It is untenable for Palestinians to live in squalor and occupation. And the current situation offers no prospect that life will improve. Israeli citizens will continue to be victimized by terrorists, and so Israel will continue to defend herself. And the situation of the Palestinian people will grow more and more miserable.

A New Palestinian Leadership

My vision is two states, living side by side in peace and security. There is simply no way to achieve that peace until all parties fight terror. Yet, at this critical moment, if all parties will break with the past and set out on a new path, we can overcome the darkness with the light of hope. Peace requires a new and different Palestinian leadership, so that a Palestinian state can be born.

I call on the Palestinian people to elect new leaders, leaders not compromised by terror. I call upon them to build a practicing democracy, based on tolerance and liberty. If the Palestinian people actively pursue these goals, America and the world will actively support their efforts. If the Palestinian people meet these goals, they will be able to reach agreement with Israel and Egypt and Jordan on security and other arrangements for independence.

And when the Palestinian people have new leaders, new institutions and new security arrangements with their neighbors, the United States of America will support the creation of a Palestinian state whose borders and certain aspects of its sovereignty will be provisional until resolved as part of a final settlement in the Middle East.

In the work ahead, we all have responsibilities. The Palestinian people are gifted and capable, and I am confident they can achieve a new birth for their nation. A Palestinian state will never be created by terror—it will be built through reform. And reform must be more than cosmetic change, or veiled attempts to preserve the status quo. True reform will require entirely new political and economic institutions, based on democracy, market economics and action against terrorism.

Today [June 24, 2002], the elected Palestinian legislature has no authority, and power is concentrated in the hands of an unaccountable few. A Palestinian state can only serve its citizens with a new constitution which separates the powers of government. The Palestinian parliament should have the full authority of a legislative body. Local officials and government ministers need authority of their own and the independence to govern effectively.

The United States, along with the European Union and Arab states, will work with Palestinian leaders to create a new constitutional framework, and a working democracy for the Palestinian people. And the United States, along with others in the international community, will help the Palestinians organize and monitor fair, multi-party local elections by the end of the year, with national elections to follow.

Today, the Palestinian people live in economic stagnation, made worse by official corruption. A Palestinian state will require a vibrant economy, where honest enterprise is encouraged by honest government. The United States, the international donor community and the World Bank stand ready to work with Palestinians on a major project of economic reform and development. The United States, the EU, the World Bank, the International Monetary Fund are willing to oversee reforms in Palestinian finances, encouraging transparency and independent auditing.

And the United States, along with our partners in the developed world, will increase our humanitarian assistance to relieve Palestinian suffering. Today, the Palestinian people lack effective courts of law and have no means to defend and vindicate their rights. A Palestinian state will require a system of reliable justice to punish those who prey on the innocent. The United States and members of the international community stand ready to work with Palestinian leaders to establish finance—establish finance and monitor a truly independent judiciary.

Support of Terrorism Is Unacceptable

Today, Palestinian authorities are encouraging, not opposing, terrorism. This is unacceptable. And the United States will not support the establishment of a Palestinian state until its leaders engage in a sustained fight against the terrorists and dismantle their infrastructure. This will require an externally supervised effort to rebuild and reform the Palestinian security services. The security system must have clear lines of authority and accountability and a unified chain of command.

America is pursuing this reform along with key regional states. The world is prepared to help, yet ultimately these steps toward statehood depend on the Palestinian people and their leaders. If they energetically take the path of reform, the rewards can come quickly. If Palestinians embrace democracy, confront corruption and firmly reject terror, they can count on American support for the creation of a provisional state of Palestine.

Setting Conditions

As for the Palestinians, their leaders (and those of the Arab states) have been entreating us for decades to press the Israelis on their behalf, and we have done so. But not until this summer [2002] has an American president set even minimal conditions on our mediation. What President [George W.] Bush has decided is that the United States cannot be an honest mediator so long as one of the parties to the conflict consists of mendacious murderers. If they want the United States to be their facilitator, they must abide by American terms. Otherwise, they're on their own.

Martin Peretz, *New Republic*, September 9, 2002.

With a dedicated effort, this state could rise rapidly, as it comes to terms with Israel, Egypt and Jordan on practical issues, such as security. The final borders, the capital and other aspects of this state's sovereignty will be negotiated between the parties, as part of a final settlement. Arab states have offered their help in this process, and their help is needed.

I've said in the past that nations are either with us or against us in the war on terror. To be counted on the side of peace, nations must act. Every leader actually committed to peace will end incitement to violence in official media, and publicly denounce homicide bombings. Every nation actually committed to peace will stop the flow of money, equipment and recruits to terrorist groups seeking the destruction of Israel—including Hamas, Islamic Jihad, and Hezbollah. Every nation actually committed to peace must block the shipment of Iranian supplies to these groups, and oppose regimes that promote terror, like Iraq. And Syria must choose the right side in the war on terror by closing terrorist camps and expelling terrorist organizations.

Leaders who want to be included in the peace process must show by their deeds an undivided support for peace. And as we move toward a peaceful solution, Arab states will be expected to build closer ties of diplomacy and commerce with Israel, leading to full normalization of relations between Israel and the entire Arab world.

Israel's Stake

Israel also has a large stake in the success of a democratic Palestine. Permanent occupation threatens Israel's identity and democracy. A stable, peaceful Palestinian state is necessary to achieve the security that Israel longs for. So I challenge Israel to take concrete steps to support the emergence of a viable, credible Palestinian state.

As we make progress towards security, Israeli forces need to withdraw fully to positions they held prior to September 28, 2000.[1] And consistent with the recommendations of the Mitchell Committee,[2] Israeli settlement activity in the occupied territories must stop.

The Palestinian economy must be allowed to develop. As violence subsides, freedom of movement should be restored, permitting innocent Palestinians to resume work and normal life. Palestinian legislators and officials, humanitarian and international workers, must be allowed to go about the business of building a better future. And Israel should release frozen

---

1. On September 28, 2000, Israeli politician Ariel Sharon made a controversial visit to a Jerusalem site holy to both Muslims and Jews, sparking a renewed wave of Palestinian violence. In response, Israel's military reoccupied parts of Gaza and the West Bank that had previously been under limited Palestinian self-rule.   2. A bipartisan commission headed by former U.S. senator George Mitchell.

Palestinian revenues into honest, accountable hands.

I've asked Secretary [of State Colin] Powell to work intensively with Middle Eastern and international leaders to realize the vision of a Palestinian state, focusing them on a comprehensive plan to support Palestinian reform and institution-building.

Ultimately, Israelis and Palestinians must address the core issues that divide them if there is to be a real peace, resolving all claims and ending the conflict between them. This means that the Israeli occupation that began in 1967 will be ended through a settlement negotiated between the parties, based on U.N. Resolutions 242 and 338,[3] with Israeli withdrawal to secure and recognize borders.

We must also resolve questions concerning Jerusalem, the plight and future of Palestinian refugees, and a final peace between Israel and Lebanon, and Israel and a Syria that supports peace and fights terror.

Peace Is Possible

All who are familiar with the history of the Middle East realize that there may be setbacks in this process. Trained and determined killers, as we have seen, want to stop it. Yet the Egyptian and Jordanian peace treaties with Israel remind us that with determined and responsible leadership progress can come quickly.

As new Palestinian institutions and new leaders emerge, demonstrating real performance on security and reform, I expect Israel to respond and work toward a final status agreement. With intensive effort by all, this agreement could be reached within three years from now. And I and my country will actively lead toward that goal.

I can understand the deep anger and anguish of the Israeli people. You've lived too long with fear and funerals, having to avoid markets and public transportation, and forced to put armed guards in kindergarten classrooms. The Palestinian

---

3. Resolution 242, passed after the 1967 war, called for the return of territories occupied in that conflict and the recognition of all states in the Middle East to exist in secure and recognized boundaries. Resolution 338, passed in 1973, called for a cease-fire in the 1973 war between Egypt and Israel and the implementation of Resolution 242.

Authority has rejected your offer at hand, and trafficked with terrorists. You have a right to a normal life; you have a right to security; and I deeply believe that you need a reformed, responsible Palestinian partner to achieve that security.

I can understand the deep anger and despair of the Palestinian people. For decades you've been treated as pawns in the Middle East conflict. Your interests have been held hostage to a comprehensive peace agreement that never seems to come, as your lives get worse year by year. You deserve democracy and the rule of law. You deserve an open society and a thriving economy. You deserve a life of hope for your children. An end to occupation and a peaceful democratic Palestinian state may seem distant, but America and our partners throughout the world stand ready to help, help you make them possible as soon as possible.

If liberty can blossom in the rocky soil of the West Bank and Gaza, it will inspire millions of men and women around the globe who are equally weary of poverty and oppression, equally entitled to the benefits of democratic government.

Universal Hopes

I have a hope for the people of Muslim countries. Your commitments to morality, and learning, and tolerance led to great historical achievements. And those values are alive in the Islamic world today. You have a rich culture, and you share the aspirations of men and women in every culture. Prosperity and freedom and dignity are not just American hopes, or Western hopes. They are universal, human hopes. And even in the violence and turmoil of the Middle East, America believes those hopes have the power to transform lives and nations.

This moment is both an opportunity and a test for all parties in the Middle East: an opportunity to lay the foundations for future peace; a test to show who is serious about peace and who is not. The choice here is stark and simple. The Bible says, "I have set before you life and death; therefore, choose life." The time has arrived for everyone in this conflict to choose peace, and hope, and life.

| *"Palestinian reforms will not end the conflict, because Palestinian politics is not the source of the conflict."*

A New Palestinian Leadership Is Not a Necessary Precondition for Peace

Wendy Pearlman

In a June 24, 2002, speech, U.S. president George W. Bush stated that progress toward a peaceful resolution of the Israel/Palestinian conflict was dependent on the Palestinian people freely electing new leadership that would crack down on terrorist acts. The idea that new Palestinian leadership is a necessary precondition for peace is questioned in the following viewpoint by Wendy Pearlman, in which she describes her involvement in translating a constitution for the Palestinians. The obstacles to peace are not the lack of Palestinian democratic or free-market institutions, she argues, but Israel's occupation of Palestinian territory and oppression of the Palestinian people. Pearlman is the author of *Occupied Voices: Stories of Loss and Longing from the Second Intifada*.

As you read, consider the following questions:

1. What event happened about the time Pearlman was finishing her work on the Palestinian constitution?
2. Why does the author believe that Palestinian democracy is irrelevant to settling the Israeli/Palestinian conflict?
3. What actions by Israel are necessary to achieve peace, according to Pearlman?

P resident [George W.] Bush's [June 24, 2002] speech on Palestinian reforms included several astute observations. The president was right to note that the "Palestinian Legislature has no authority and power is concentrated in the hands of an unaccountable few." Palestinian legislators, after all, are trapped under military curfew. Power over all aspects of Palestinians' lives is in the hands of the Israeli prime minister, who is unaccountable to international law, no less to the 3 million Palestinian civilians who suffer an unrelenting siege.

And the president was also right to remark, "the Palestinian people lack effective courts of law and have no means to defend and vindicate their rights." The Israeli army, after all, has rounded up thousands of Palestinians without charge or trial. They endure inhuman conditions and languish in Israeli prisons indefinitely.

But the president was misinformed when he told the Palestinians to draft a democratic constitution. The Palestinians already have such a constitution. I know, because I translated it.

Palestine's Constitution

[Palestinian leader] Yasser Arafat established a Constitution Committee in 1999, long before either George Bush or [Israeli prime minister] Ariel Sharon came to power and assumed the right to tell Palestinians how to run their affairs. After months of research and debate, the Committee completed a draft in September 2000. Two friends and I, all three of us students of Arabic sharing an apartment in Cairo, were asked to translate the draft. We eagerly agreed.

For days on end, we hovered around my laptop, meticulously considering every word we translated. As modern twenty-something women, we were determined to make the Palestinian constitution even more democratic than the American one by rendering the English text gender-neutral. Not unlike male politicians and academics everywhere, however, the members of the Palestinian Constitution Committee eventually reinserted the he's that we had taken such pains to circumvent.

So I've reviewed every "for," "if," and "but" of the Palestinian Constitution, and I can say that it's not too bad. It provides for regular elections, separation of powers, and civil rights. It addresses the rights of Palestinian refugees, and it pledges religious tolerance. Granted, the constitution is far from perfect. Palestinian human rights activists have called attention to loopholes that grant the executive branch the wide discretion that it enjoys throughout the developing world. More than grounds for invalidating the current draft, however, this debate illustrates that democratic dialogue is alive and well in Palestinian civil society.

Change Must Come from Within

If we are serious about reform in the Palestinian Authority, then we must allow the Palestinians and the Arabs to deal with [Yasser] Arafat. Credible alternative Palestinian leadership will not step forward in response to a perceived American-Israeli demand for Arafat's removal. Change must come from within. . . .

The United States must lead a diplomatic process to break the endless cycle of violence and get to the end game—an independent Palestinian state and security for Israel. We cannot wait until Palestine is a full-blown Jeffersonian democracy before getting on with a peace process.

Chuck Hagel, *Washington Post*, July 19, 2002.

My friends and I became completely absorbed in the constitution of the Palestinian state-to-be in order to meet our Sept. 30, 2000, deadline.

Renewed Violence

It was only after we had submitted our translation, therefore, that we switched on the news and discovered that Palestine was in flames. Two days before, Ariel Sharon had visited the Al-Aqsa mosque. Clashes had ensued between Palestinian protesters and Israeli police the next day. According to the Palestinian Red Crescent, some 60 Palestinians were killed and 2,500 injured during the week following Sharon's visit. Within a month, another 125 Palestinians would be killed. The 126th to die was this intifada's first suicide bomber. The rest is history.

The three of us spent weeks in our Cairo apartment consumed by the news from Palestine. Listening to the reports about the bombing of neighborhoods, demolition of homes, and countless funerals, we would exclaim, "How can this happen? The Palestinians have a constitution!" We knew then what our president still does not understand. A Palestinian constitution means little as long as the Israeli occupation continues.

Palestinian reforms will not end the conflict, because Palestinian politics is not the source of the conflict. The violence will not end until Israel takes its soldiers and settlers and leaves the West Bank and Gaza, once and for all.

Democracy in Palestine Is Beside the Point

President Bush's call for democracy in Palestine, therefore, is not wrong as much as it is beside the point. It does not matter how the Palestinians choose their leaders when Israel retains the power to besiege, arrest, or assassinate them. It does not matter what free-market institutions the Palestinians develop as long as Israel can [bring] commerce, not to mention all daily life, to a screeching halt.

Israel is wreaking havoc in Palestinian towns and refugee camps with impunity, and the White House's solution is to audit the PNA [Palestine National Authority]? Perhaps the president got the Enron and Middle East files mixed up. His speech reads more like a prescription for reforming American finance than a vision for a just resolution to the Palestinians' 50-year struggle for statehood.

The Palestinians already have a constitution; they don't need another one. What they need is to be treated like a people.

*"The fence would be no uglier than the
reality it seeks to control."*

A Fence Separating Israelis and
Palestinians Can Create Peace

Richard Cohen

In 1996 Israel's internal security minister, Moshe Shahal,
proposed the creation of a fence that would separate Israel
from Palestinians in the West Bank. Since then, a growing
number of Israelis have supported this idea, and construction of such a fence was started in 2002. In the following
viewpoint, *Washington Post* columnist Richard Cohen evalu-
ates whether a "separation fence" is desirable. Such a structure, he argues, would help prevent attacks against Israel and
help quell conflict in the region. Without such a fence, he
contends, Israel will remain vulnerable to suicidal terrorists.

As you read, consider the following questions:
1. What oxymoron does Cohen use to begin the article?
2. What does the author state he cannot understand about
   Palestinians?
3. What comparison does Cohen make between the West
   Bank and Gaza?

An oxymoron is a contradiction in terms. Here are some humorous ones: military justice, airline food. Here's one that's not so funny: Israeli suicide bomber.

The absurdity of the term alerts you instantly to the nature of the Palestinian-Israeli struggle. It's a clash of cultures. One side could never use suicide bombers; the other serves them up on almost a daily basis. One side has soldiers who weep over the bodies of their dead comrades; the other has fighters who transform death into a political statement so that every funeral is a rally.

A Separating Fence

Ehud Barak, the former Israeli prime minister, is among those who recommend that a fence be erected to separate the two peoples. It is a capital idea—not a long-term solution, not a peace plan and, of course, not a beautiful sight for the world's TV cameras. Such a fence could separate Palestinians from Jews on the West Bank and those areas of it—the Jerusalem suburbs, for instance—that are destined to remain part of Israel for the foreseeable future. The fence would be no uglier than the reality it seeks to control.

This fence would take its place with its historical predecessors—the Great Wall of China or the one the Roman Emperor Hadrian had built across the north of England. It ran 73 miles and was designed to keep out the "barbarians"—a word that nowadays you have to put in quotation marks, since it is forbidden to consider one culture inferior to another. So without getting into value judgments, let us just stipulate that Palestinian and Israeli cultures are different—and that difference requires a fence.

The difference is encapsulated in the chirpy remark of Khalil Takafka, whose daughter, Andaleeb, had just blown up herself and six others at Jerusalem's Mahane Yehuda market. "I am happy," he said. "All girls should do it." His daughter was 20.

I understand. I understand the political situation, the frustration, the humiliation of the Israeli occupation. I have seen it firsthand. I understand the lack of hope, how dim the future is and the hate for the Israelis, who not only have the biggest guns but a swaggering know-how. I understand.

But I do not understand the celebration over the loss of life—the newspaper notices placed by the proud family of the martyrdom of their son or daughter. I do not understand the lack of bitter regret or grudging reluctance to accept the tactic and, instead, a joyful embrace of suicide-cum-homicide, even when the victims are children, pregnant women or the old. The best—the only—thing that can be said of such tactics is that they work. Indeed, they do.

An Israeli Writer Endorses Separation

Since neither [the Palestinians] nor we are at present capable of reaching [a peace agreement] . . . regarding the permanent border, it is imperative that we set this border ourselves, temporarily, and withdraw from part of the territories, including the many remote settlements that preclude any possibility of drawing this border.

A border will protect us better against destructive suicide bombers, and will assist the saner elements in the Palestinian camp to stop them before they reach us, thus restricting the vicious cycle of their terror and our counter-attack. Unilateral withdrawal will make curfews, closures and roadblocks unnecessary, along with the daily suffering they cause the Palestinian population, and will prevent loss of life among the settlers and the soldiers charged with protecting them.

This partial, unilateral withdrawal will also debunk the false myth that the Arabs have subscribed to since the early days of Zionism, the myth of the Jew coming to rob their lands from the Nile to the Tigris. The image of the borderless Jew will become that of the Israeli within borders.

I am not so naive as to think that this will bring immediate peace. . . .

But this path will enable us at least to free ourselves partially from the suicidal Palestinian embrace while we wait for them to come to their senses. There are some indications that this is happening; the seeds of Palestinian self-criticism give us hope.

Avraham B. Yehoshua, *Jerusalem Evening Post*, July 19, 2002.

So the fence. There is one between Israel and the Gaza Strip. Anyone who has been there can tell you that the West Bank is Eden by comparison. Gaza is poor. Gaza is a mess. In Gaza, 78 percent of the residents approve of suicide bombings. Yet few suicide bombers have come from Gaza. The reason? The fence.

Conventional wisdom has it that Israel is the dominant power in the region. Conventionally speaking, that's true. But in an interview with my *Washington Post* colleague Lee Hockstader, a senior Hamas official identified Israel's Achilles' heel. "Anyone reading an Israeli newspaper can see their suffering," said Ismail Haniya. Jews "love life" more than any other people, he said.

Well, I don't know about any other people, but I do know that Jews would never send their young out to blow themselves up and kill innocent people in the process. I do know that they are culturally incapable of such behavior—although, for sure, here and there a crazed zealot exists. . . .

Good Fences Make Good Neighbors

Occupation powers do tough, mean things, and Israel has done them. Israel ought to get out of the West Bank, get out of the settlements—and get a prime minister who at least believes in the peace process and is not a walking, talking provocation to the Palestinians.

But as quickly as it can, it ought to build that fence, unilaterally disengaging from the Palestinians. What Robert Frost said about a New England wall applies to a Middle East fence. It would make for good neighbors.

"Israel must not be tempted by the fiction of security behind a wall."

A Fence Between Israelis and Palestinians Will Not Create Peace

David Grossman

Responding to months of conflict and terrorist attacks, some Israeli leaders have proposed the option of "unilateral separation" between Israelis and Palestinians. They argue that by enforcing such a separation with walls, fences, and surveillance systems between Israel and areas under the limited self-rule of the Palestinian Authority, terrorist attacks could be prevented and conflict reduced. On June 17, 2002, construction began on a 217-mile fence between Israel and the West Bank. In the following viewpoint, Israeli author and peace activist David Grossman argues that although a secure border between Israel and Palestine is necessary, constructing this wall without first reaching a peace agreement with the Palestinians will provide only a temporary illusion of peace and security for Israel. The fence will only encourage those on both sides of the conflict to give up any efforts to reach a negotiated peace, and may cause increased unrest among Israel's Arab citizens, he contends.

As you read, consider the following questions:

1. What military problems does Grossman foresee arising from the security fence?
2. How is Israel hurting itself in peace negotiations by constructing a wall, according to the author?
3. Why do many Israelis support a fence, according to Grossman?

David Grossman, "Illusions of a Separate Peace," *The New York Times*, July 12, 2002. Copyright © 2002 by The New York Times Company. Reproduced by permission.

As you read this [in July 2002], a fence is going up to sep-arate Israel from Palestinians. For now, it is defined as temporary, for defensive purposes only. It encompasses, on its Israeli side, most of the settlements Israel has established in the occupied territories. It is not intended to determine the future border between Israel and the Palestinian Authority.

"Good fences make good neighbors," wrote the poet Robert Frost. Israel and Palestine are certainly not good neighbors, and there is an urgent need, both in practice and in principle, to establish a border between them. I mean a border with defensive and barrier devices, open only at crossings established by mutual consent. Such a border will protect the two sides from each other, help stabilize their re-lations and, especially, require them to internalize, once and for all, the concept of a border. It's a vague, elusive and prob-lematic concept for both, since they've lived for the last 100 years without clear boundaries, with constant invasion, each within, on top of, over and under the other.

A Temporary Illusion of Security

Yet it is very dangerous to establish such a border fence right now, unilaterally, without a peace agreement. It is yet another precipitate action aimed at giving the Israeli public a tempo-rary illusion of security; its main effect will be to supply Is-raelis with a counterfeit replacement for a peace process.

There may well come a time—after both sides have at-tempted another serious and sincere move toward peace—when Israel will conclude that there really is no chance of peace in this generation. In such a case, Israel will have to withdraw from the occupied territories, evacuate almost all the settlements, shut itself behind a thick wall and prepare for an ongoing battle.

From my conversations with Palestinian leaders, however, I am convinced there still is a chance for peace. Most Israelis disagree. "There's no one to make an agreement with!" they say. "Even [former Israeli prime minister] Shimon Peres and the leaders of the left say that they are no longer willing to talk with [Palestinian leader Yasser] Arafat, and in the mean-time Israel must defend itself against terror somehow!"

But even if we assume that Yasir Arafat is not a negotiating partner—by the way, it certainly hasn't been proved that [Israeli prime minister] Ariel Sharon is a partner—we need to examine the practical implications of building a barrier fence without an agreement. It is clear to everyone that such a fence will not prevent, for example, the Palestinians' firing rockets and mortars from their territory into Israel. The Israeli Army will have to operate beyond the fence, in order to defend isolated Israeli settlements that will remain on the other side. It takes little imagination to realize what military complications this will bring.

The fence will not provide an appropriate military response to the complex situation in Jerusalem, in which Jews and Arabs rub shoulders each day. Quite the opposite. An attempt to detach East Jerusalem from the rest of the Palestinian territories is liable to turn the Arab city's inhabitants to the use of terror, which they have mostly resisted so far.

The distress Israelis feel is plain and comprehensible. It derives from the inhuman cruelty of the suicide bombings and from the feeling that there is no way out, given the huge support for terrorism among Palestinians. But this distress cannot overcome my sense that the Israeli infatuation with the fence is the product of a psychological need. It is not a well-considered policy.

Sacrificing Negotiating Positions

In establishing a fence unilaterally, Israel is throwing away the best card it has. It will be discarding this trump without receiving anything in return from the Palestinians. Last month [June 2002] in London, I heard Yasir Abed Rabbo, the Palestinian information minister, say in a conversation with Israelis from the peace camp that if Israel withdraws behind a fence, Palestinians will spend a day celebrating that most of the occupation has ended, and the next day will continue the intifada, in order to obtain the rest of their demands.

Those other demands are well known: Israeli withdrawal from 100 percent of the territories Israel occupied in the 1967 war; evacuation of all the [Jewish West Bank] settlements; Arab Jerusalem as the capital of Palestine; and acceptance of the principle of the Palestinian refugees' right of return within Israel proper.

Yet there is today a good chance of resolving all these issues in negotiations. . . . But if the demands of Palestinians are not resolved in negotiations, the fighting will continue. In fact, Palestinians may fight more fiercely if they feel their terror has forced Israel into a new ghetto.

A Palestinian View

To Palestinians, the proposals for unilateral separation are just another form of maintaining the Israeli occupation on certain parts of the Palestinian territories. They are also perceived as a way for Israel to unilaterally determine the future of the relationship between the two sides—boxing Palestinians in on "their" side, without access to resources and divided by Israeli settlements and areas of control. . . .

Those who hope that plans for separation would move us closer towards peace, or even calm the currently fierce struggle against occupation and the Israeli violence used to maintain that occupation, will be sorely mistaken. Plans for unilateral separation leave certain parts of the Palestinian territories under occupation, do not solve the issue of Jerusalem and do not bring closure to the problem of the Palestinian refugees. These are major components of the conflict that must be addressed and agreed upon with the support of international legality and in a way that is acceptable to both sides.

What proponents of unilateral separation hope is that if the two peoples become invisible to one another, their conflict will diminish. But the conflict cannot be taken care of by shutting the door on Palestinians.

Ghassan Khatib, *bitterlemons.org*, April 2, 2002.

Because it is so important, let me say it again: the establishment of a fence without an agreement means Israel will give up most of the occupied territories without the Palestinians giving up the right of return.

Palestinians in Israel

The establishment of a fence without peace also means that the fence will have to extend into the West Bank to encompass most of the settlements. But in building the fence to include the settlements, Israel will have to take in many Palestinian towns and villages that lie close to the settlements and to the roads that lead to them. According to some estimates, this will involve about 150,000 Palestinians. If we add the Arabs of East Jerusalem, the number of Palestinians on the Israeli side of the fence may well reach 400,000.

These people will not be Israeli citizens. Israel does not want them. They will have no clear legal status and will not be able to participate in elections. Does anyone seriously believe they will not turn to terrorism? When that happens, they will be inside the fence, not outside it, and they will have unobstructed passage to Israel's city centers. Or will Israel confine them behind yet another, second fence?

Israel correctly fears giving Palestinians the right of return to within its borders. So it is hard to understand how Israel could be prepared to take in hundreds of thousands of hostile Palestinians by building a fence.

Another question: How will Israel's Arab citizens feel? They are about a sixth of the population. Many have ties to families in the Palestinian Authority lands. Will these ties be severed by the fence? Will Israel not be increasing the bitterness and frustration of this one-sixth of the citizenry, and will not this lead Israeli Arabs to adopt even more extreme positions at a time when their connection to their country has been growing more tenuous?

The fence's major drawing power for most Israelis is that it has never been tried. So it can be believed in, for a while.

The Luxury of Despair

But the border between Israel and Palestine can be set only through full agreement by both sides. Such an agreement seems impossible today, but we cannot allow ourselves the luxury of despairing of it. I think it's better to wait and live for a few more years without this fence of illusions. This wall will declare our absolute despair of reaching a peace agreement in our generation, of integrating a normal Israel into the region around it.

A wall will allow the extremists—who are all too numerous—to argue that there will be no one to talk to in the future. Putting the other out of sight will only make dehumanization easier and justify a more extreme struggle.

Israel must not be tempted by the fiction of security behind a wall. Instead, it must invest its energy in the recommencement of negotiations. If Mr. Arafat is unacceptable to Mr. Sharon and Mr. Bush, let those leaders explain to us how they can create a better situation. Until they can do so, they bear the responsibility—no less weighty than Mr. Arafat's responsibility—for the immobility, the insensibility and the despair on both sides.

Periodical Bibliography

The following articles have been selected to supplement the diverse views presented in this chapter.

Hady Amr	"How Can Bullets and Bombs Bring Peace? Palestinians Have Cause for Grievance, but the World Won't Listen Until They Return to Nonviolent Protest," *Newsweek*, March 11, 2002.
David Arnow	"Voices of Reconciliation in a Time of Hatred," *Tikkun*, March/April 2001.
Shlomo Avineri	"Irreconcilable Differences: The Best Solution to the Israeli-Palestinian Conflict Might Be No Solution at All," *Foreign Policy*, March 2002.
Mubarak Awad and Abdul Aziz	"The Road to Arab-Israeli Peace," *Tikkun*, January/February 2001.
Aluf Benn	"The Last of the Patriarchs," *Foreign Affairs*, May/June 2002.
Current Events	"Mideast Meltdown: Fighting Intensifies Between Israelis and Palestinians," April 5, 2002.
Economist	"The Dangers of Leaving It to Sharon; America, Israel, and the Palestinians," February 2, 2002.
Yuval Elizur	"Israel Banks on a Fence," *Foreign Affairs*, March/April 2003.
Mordechai Gafni	"Do Not Ask Israel to Atone," *Tikkun*, January/February 2001.
Ronald L. Hatchett	"The Importance of the Saudi Peace Plan," *World & I*, June 2002.
Tony Judt	"The Road to Nowhere," *New York Review of Books*, May 9, 2002.
James Kitfield	"The Ties That Bind, and Constrain: The Mideast," *National Journal*, April 20, 2002.
Anthony Lewis	"Is There a Solution?" *New York Review of Books*, April 25, 2002.
Johanna McGeary	"The Four Sticking Points: Peace Will Never Be Achieved Unless Israel and the Palestinians Compromise on Some Extremely Tough Issues," *Time*, April 22, 2002.
Jerome Slater	"What Went Wrong?" The Collapse of the Israeli-Palestinian Peace Process," *Political Science Quarterly*, Summer 2001.

Time   "Israel's Last-Ditch Peace Plan: Exhausted by
                          Violence, Israel's Politicians Consider a Radical
                          Move. Is It Time for Economic Separation?"
                          November 6, 2000.

James M. Wall   "Numb About Israel," *Christian Century*, March
                          27, 2002.

For Further Discussion

Chapter 1

1. Efraim Karsh argues that Palestinians and outsiders have different conceptions of the word *occupation*. Why does he consider it important to clarify the differing meanings of such terms as *occupation* and *occupied territories*? Do you agree that such delineation is necessary? Explain.

2. William O. Beeman's argument that Middle East conflict is in part created by the United States and other nations is presented in the context of assessing America's "war on terrorism" following the September 11, 2001, attacks. What does he recommend the United States do to respond to the attacks? Do you agree or disagree with his view that military attacks would not work?

3. The authors of this chapter discuss several causes of tension and potential conflict in the Middle East. After reading this chapter, what do you believe is the predominant source of conflict in the region? Support your answer with evidence from the viewpoints.

Chapter 2

1. Ray Takeyh argues that future Islamic democracies may well contain elements of Western democracies, but they would also be different in important ways; for example, Islamic democracies may impose more limits on individual freedoms. Takeyh argues against a "single universal standard" of human rights. Do you agree or disagree with this position? Could an Islamic nation adopt just some elements of Western democracies and still be considered true democracies? Defend your answer.

2. After reading the articles by Takeyh and Milton Viorst, do you think that the Middle East will be more democratic in ten years? In fifty? Or are such predictions inherently suspect? Explain, citing examples from both texts.

3. Martin Kramer contends that fundamentalist Islam's drive for power often mobilizes its adherents for violent conflict. Muhammad M. El-Hodaiby argues that a Muslim who participates in violence is committing a sin because Islamic tenets explicitly reject violence. Kramer was the director of a Middle Eastern studies program at an Israeli university; El-Hodaiby is a leader of the Muslim Brotherhood in Egypt. Does knowing

their backgrounds influence your assessment of their arguments? Explain your answer.

Chapter 3

1. Leon T. Hadar argues that the United States has no compelling reason to intervene to end the Arab-Israeli conflict. Is his contention addressed in Sherwin Wine's article? What, if any, American national interests do you believe may justify American intervention in the Middle East? Defend your answer.

2. After reading the articles by Wine and Hadar, how much influence do you believe the United States has in the Middle East? Could the United States impose a peace agreement to end the Arab-Israeli conflict if it really wanted to? Explain.

3. Both Victor Davis Hanson and Marina Ottway and her coauthors argue that building democracy in the Middle East will be a long and difficult process. What is their main area of disagreement? Who do you believe makes the more convincing argument? Defend your answer.

4. After reading the viewpoints by the *Ellsworth American* and *Christian Century*, and by Diane Katz and Henry Payne, do you think America's dependency on Middle East oil is a serious problem? Explain, citing from the viewpoints.

5. After reading the viewpoints in this chapter, identify what you believe to be America's leading interests and concerns in the Middle East. Which do you consider most important? Defend your rankings.

Chapter 4

1. Many of the arguments against Israeli-Palestinian peace negotiations focus on the credibility of Yasir (Yasser) Arafat. Arafat contends that such personal attacks are not relevant nor are they conducive to the peace process. Do you believe such personal attacks raise a legitimate point, given Arafat's position as leader of the Palestinians? Explain your answer.

2. Some critics of George W. Bush argue that the demands he makes on the Palestinians are not balanced by equivalent demands on Israel. After reading the viewpoints by Bush and by Wendy Pearlman, do you agree with this assessment? What additional demands, if any, on either Palestine or Israel, would you consider as a precondition to peace talks?

3. What comparison does Richard Cohen make between the Israelis and the Palestinians? Do you agree or disagree with his assessment of the nature of the Palestinian people? Why or why not?

4. After reading the arguments of Cohen and David Grossman, do you believe a separation fence would be a feasible short-term solution for the Israeli-Palestinian conflict? A good long-term solution? What would you consider to be the major advantages and disadvantages of unilateral separation?

Chronology of Events

1897	Theodor Herzl convenes First Zionist Congress, which designates Palestine as an appropriate Jewish homeland. Less than 10 percent of Palestine's population is Jewish.
1914–1918	World War I. Arab nationalists cooperate with Britain against Turkey. Turkey's Ottoman Empire collapses.
1917	British foreign secretary A.J. Balfour declares Britain's support for a national homeland for the Jewish people in Palestine, a declaration that conflicts with promises to the Arabs.
1920–1948	Britain rules Palestine under agreement with the League of Nations. The British mandate approves limited immigration for Jews.
1921	Military officer Reza Khan rules Iran after a coup and begins a secularization campaign that abolishes many Islamic customs. Faisal I, with British support, is made king of Iraq, which is composed of three former Ottoman Empire provinces.
1922	At the Uqair Conference, the modern borders of Iraq, Saudi Arabia, and Kuwait are drawn by representatives of the British government.
1927–1938	Oil is discovered in commercial quantities in northern Iraq, Bahrain, Saudi Arabia, and Kuwait.
1928	The Muslim Brotherhood is established in Egypt as a movement of fundamentalist reform among Sunni Muslims.
1929–1939	Arabs rebel against British rule; Arabs fight Jews for the right to live in Palestine.
1939–1945	World War II. Six million Jews are killed by Nazi Germany. Jewish population in Palestine swells to 608,000 by 1946.
1941	British and Soviet forces, concerned that Reza Khan is allied with Adolf Hitler, invade Iran and depose the monarch, replacing him with his son, Muhammed Reza Khan Pahlavi.
November 1943	Lebanon achieves independence, with government posts given to members of each of the main religious groups.
November 29, 1947	United Nations (UN) General Assembly votes to partition Palestine into Jewish and Arab states with Jerusalem being an international city. Arabs refuse.

May 14, 1948	David Ben-Gurion proclaims the state of Israel, which is immediately attacked by five Arab states. Israel defeats the coalition, and takes more land than originally assigned. More than 500,000 Palestinians flee Israel.
1952	Officers of the Egyptian army overthrow King Farouk and replace him with their leader, Gamal Abdel Nasser.
1953	U.S. and British intelligence forces organize a coup against democratic reformer Muhammed Mossadeq that restores the Shah of Iran, Muhammed Reza Pahlavi, to power. He allows a consortium of foreign companies to operate Iran's oil industry.
July 1956	The U.S. and Britain refuse to support a loan to Egypt to build the Aswan High Dam; in retaliation, Nasser seizes control of the Suez Canal. After Britain freezes Egyptian assets held in England, Egypt closes the canal.
October 1956	The Israelis, with military aid from Britain and France, invade Egypt. They take the Gaza Strip and the Sinai Peninsula, which they later return in a peace settlement.
1958	Faisal II, who had succeeded Faisal I as king of Iraq, is assassinated. Abdul Karim Kassem installs himself as military dictator of Iraq.
August 1959	Jordan offers citizenship to all Palestinian refugees.
January 1961	Iran, Iraq, Kuwait, and Saudi Arabia found the Organization of Petroleum Exporting Countries (OPEC).
May 1964	Palestine Liberation Organization (PLO) is established.
May 1967	Nasser orders UN emergency forces to withdraw from the Sinai, declares a state of emergency in the Gaza Strip, and closes the Strait of Tiran to shipping to and from Israel. Israel and the U.S warn Egypt to remove the blockade.
June 5–10, 1967	Six-Day War. Israel attacks Egypt, Jordan, and Syria and captures the Sinai, Gaza Strip, West Bank, and Golan Heights.
November 22, 1967	UN Security Council Resolution 242 calling for peace in the Middle East is adopted. The resolution asks that Israel return land acquired in the Six-Day War and that Arabs respect Israel's boundaries.
1969	Yasser Arafat and Fatah (the largest Palestinian group) take over the PLO and give it a more assertive role.

1970	Nasser dies and Vice President Anwar Sadat takes over leadership of Egypt.
1970–1971	Jordanian civil war. King Hussein crushes Palestinian guerrillas and invading troops. Palestinians move offices from Jordan to Beirut, Lebanon.
October 6, 1973	Yom Kippur War. Egypt and Syria launch a two-front surprise attack on Israeli forces in the Sinai Peninsula and the Golan Heights.
October 18, 1973	First day of five-month Arab oil embargo cutting off or sharply curtailing oil exports to countries that support Israel.
November 11, 1973	Egypt and Israel agree to a cease-fire.
October 1974	The UN grants the PLO observer status and allows it to participate in debates on the status of Palestinian refugees.
April 1975	In Lebanon, Christian Phalangists attack Palestinians, touching off large-scale confrontations between Christians and Muslims. Syria participates on the side of the Muslims.
November 1977	Sadat makes the first visit of an Arab leader to Israel to promote renewed peace talks. In exchange for peace, Israel offers to return Sinai to Egypt and allow limited Palestinian self-rule in the Israeli-occupied areas of the West Bank and Gaza Strip.
September 1978	Camp David summit meeting between U.S. president Jimmy Carter, Israeli prime minister Menachem Begin, and Sadat leads to an Egyptian-Israeli peace agreement and accords on the Palestinian question. Under the agreement, Israel returns all of Sinai to Egypt by 1982. Most of the Arab states, the Soviet Union, and the PLO denounce the agreements.
February 1979	After months of unrest, the government of Iran is overthrown. The Shah is replaced by Shi'ite Muslim fundamentalists led by Ayatollah Ruhollah Khomeini.
July 1979	Saddam Hussein seizes power in Iraq.
November 4, 1979	Militants storm the U.S. embassy in Tehran, Iran, and hold fifty-two Americans hostage for the next fourteen months.
September 1980	Iran makes air attacks on Iraqi towns. A few weeks later, Iraq invades Iran, beginning the eight-year Iran-Iraq war.
1981	Jewish settlements and housing construction on the West Bank begin.

June 1981	Israel bombs a nuclear reactor in Iraq "to prevent another Holocaust." The U.S. refuses to deliver promised military equipment to Israel.
October 1981	Sadat is assassinated by members of the Egyptian army. Vice President Hosni Mubarak takes over the government.
December 1981	Israel annexes the Golan Heights in Syria. The UN Security Council declares the annexation "null and void." Israel refuses to withdraw.
February 1982	Syrian leader Hafez Assad's troops crush a Muslim Brotherhood uprising in the city of Hama, killing more than ten thousand people.
June–September 1982	Israel invades Lebanon; it occupies Beirut and demands that the PLO leave the city. U.S. Marines help oversee the PLO evacuation. The PLO establishes its headquarters in Tunisia.
April 18, 1983	Sixty-three people are killed in the bombing of the U.S. embassy in Beirut.
May 17, 1983	Lebanon and Israel sign an agreement to withdraw Israeli forces from Lebanon. Israel refuses to withdraw completely until Syria also withdraws.
October 23, 1983	A pro-Iranian suicide bomber drives an explosives-laden truck into U.S. Marine headquarters in Beirut, killing 241 people.
January 1984	The administration of U.S. president Ronald Reagan officially lists Iran as a supporter of international terrorism and cuts arms sales to Iran.
May 16, 1985	Journalist Terry A. Anderson is kidnapped and held hostage in Lebanon. He becomes the longest-held American hostage of the eighteen kidnapped by various Islamic groups in Lebanon between 1982 and 1991. Of these eighteen hostages, three died or were killed in captivity, one escaped, six were released before 1987, two were released in 1990, and the remaining six were released in 1991.
June 1985	Shi'ite gunmen hijack TWA flight 847 and hold its 153 passengers hostage. They kill a U.S. Navy passenger. Most passengers are released except for 39 Americans, who are taken to Beirut. Iranian officials help negotiate freedom for the Americans.
October 7, 1985	Four Palestinians hijack the Italian ship *Achille Lauro* and hold 400 hostages. They kill Leon Klinghoffer, an elderly American Jew.
April 14, 1986	Reagan, arguing that Libyan leader Muammar Qaddafi supports anti-American terrorism, orders the bombing

of Libyan cities Tripoli and Benghazi. Dozens of Libyans die as many homes are hit, including Qaddafi's.

November 1986   The U.S. government reveals that it covertly sold arms to Iran and diverted profits to the Nicaraguan Contra resistance in Central America. The scandal becomes known as the Iran-Contra affair.

December 1987   Four Palestinians are killed when an Israeli army truck rams their car after they attempt to run a military road-block in Gaza. During their funeral, Israeli troops clash with mourners. The event marks the beginning of the widespread Palestinian uprising that comes to be called the *intifada*. Hundreds of demonstrators are killed over the next five years in clashes between Israelis and Palestinians.

July 3, 1988   U.S. Navy ship patrolling the Persian Gulf accidentally shoots down Iranian commercial airliner, killing 290.

August 1988   Iran and Iraq accept UN peace terms and announce a cease-fire. The eight-year war leaves more than one million casualties. 100,000 Kurds flee to Turkey amidst reports that Iraq is attacking them with poison gas.

November 1988   Palestine National Council (PNC) meets in Algiers and votes to accept UN Security Council Resolutions 242 and 338, which call for Arab recognition of Israel and Israeli withdrawal from territories occupied since 1967. Jordan severs legal and administrative ties to the West Bank. Responsibility for the West Bank's economic and municipal functions shifts to the PLO.

December 1988   The U.S. establishes a "diplomatic dialogue" with the PLO after Arafat renounces terrorism and states that he accepts the right of "Palestine, Israel, and other neighbors" to exist in peace.

February 1989   Iranian leader Khomeini calls for Muslims to execute Indian-born British author Salman Rushdie, whose novel *The Satanic Verses* Khomeini calls blasphemous.

June 3, 1989   Iranian leader Khomeini dies in Tehran.

April 2, 1990   Iraqi president Saddam Hussein claims Iraq possesses advanced chemical weapons and threatens to destroy half of Israel if it launches any preemptive strike against Iraq.

August 2, 1990   Iraq invades Kuwait. The emir of Kuwait flees to Saudi Arabia. The UN Security Council passes Resolution 660 condemning the invasion and demanding Iraq's unconditional withdrawal from Kuwait.

August 6, 1990	The UN Security Council passes Resolution 661, which imposes a trade embargo and economic sanctions on Iraq.
August 7, 1990	U.S. president George H.W. Bush, after consulting with the leaders of Great Britain, the Soviet Union, Japan, Egypt, and Saudi Arabia, sends U.S. forces to Saudi Arabia to protect it from a potential Iraqi invasion.
November 29, 1990	The UN Security Council passes Resolution 678 authorizing the use of "all necessary means" to force Iraq from Kuwait if Iraq does not withdraw before January 15, 1991.
January 16, 1991	Allied coalition forces launch massive air attacks on Iraq. Israel declares a state of emergency and imposes a curfew in the occupied territories.
January 18, 1991	Iraq attacks Israel with Scud missiles, causing light casualties. The U.S. responds by sending troops to operate Patriot anti-missile systems in Israel.
February 23, 1991	The U.S.-led multinational coalition launches a ground offensive against Iraqi troops.
February 27, 1991	Bush declares victory over Iraq and announces the liberation of Kuwait.
April 1991	The UN Security Council passes resolutions establishing a formal cease-fire between Iraq and the UN coalition and condemning Iraq's suppression of Kurds and Shi'ites. It also passes Resolution 687, requiring Iraq to destroy its weapons of mass destruction. A Special Commission on Iraq (UNSCOM) is formed to monitor Iraq's compliance with Resolution 687.
July 4, 1991	After four days of clashes around Sidon, Lebanon, the PLO agrees to withdraw from its only military base near Israel.
October 30, 1991	International Middle East peace conference is convened in Madrid, Spain. The event marks the first open and direct negotiations between Israel, Syria, Jordan, Lebanon, and the Palestinians. No treaties or agreements are signed. The participants agree to meet for further talks.
July 1992	Yitzhak Rabin is elected prime minister of Israel. He pledges to promote peace and to limit construction of new Jewish settlements in the occupied territories.
August 1992	The UN Security Council establishes "no-fly" zones in northern and southern Iraq in response to continued Iraqi air strikes on Shi'ite rebels. The areas are patrolled by U.S.-led UN troops.

February 1993	Israeli and Palestinian officials begin secret talks in Oslo, Norway. Israel agrees to withdraw from most of Gaza and the West Bank city of Jericho. Arafat's Palestinian Authority is to administer these areas. The final status of the occupied territories is to be determined over the next several years.
February 26, 1993	The World Trade Center in New York City is bombed, leaving six dead and thousands injured. A group of Middle Eastern Islamic militants, later convicted of the bombing, claim the attack was in revenge for U.S. support of Israel.
July 25, 1993	Israel begins a week-long air and artillery assault on 70 villages in southern Lebanon, killing more than 100 Lebanese and driving 300,000 refugees northward. The assault is in retaliation for rocket attacks on Israeli settlements by the pro-Iranian Hezbollah militia, stationed in Lebanon.
September 1993	Rabin and Arafat sign letters proclaiming that the PLO recognizes the right of Israel to exist in peace and security and that Israel acknowledges the PLO as the representative of the Palestinian people. In Washington, D.C., Rabin and Arafat officially sign the historic peace accords agreed to at Oslo.
1994	The Palestinian National Authority (PNA) is formed to govern the semi-autonomous Palestinian state. Violence breaks out as Jewish settlers resist efforts to turn land over to the PNA.
October 1994	54,000 U.S. troops are sent to the Middle East after Iraq again threatens to invade Kuwait. Iraq subsequently withdraws its troops from the Kuwaiti border.
September 1995	The Israeli-Palestinian Oslo II interim agreements are signed. Oslo II divides the West Bank into three areas: one section that is to be governed by the PNA, another section that is granted limited Palestinian self-rule, and a third area to remain under Israeli rule.
November 1995	A car bomb explodes outside an army training building in Riyadh, Saudi Arabia, killing five Americans and two Indians. The Saudi government captures and executes Muslim terrorists implicated in the bombing.
November 4, 1995	Yitzhak Rabin is assassinated by an ultra-right Israeli extremist. Shimon Peres takes over as Israel's prime minister.
May 1996	Benjamin Netanyahu is elected prime minister of Israel.
June 25, 1996	A truck bomb explodes outside a military apartment building in the Khobar Towers complex in Dhahran,

	Saudi Arabia, killing 19 U.S. airmen and injuring hundreds. Shi'ite terrorists are suspected in the bombing.
September 1996	Violence breaks out in Jerusalem after Israeli authorities open a tunnel near a Muslim holy site. More than 70 people die as a result of clashes involving protestors, Palestinian police, and Israeli soldiers. The U.S. launches 44 cruise missiles into Iraq in response to Iraqi attacks on Kurds in the north. The UN extends the southern no-fly zone closer to Baghdad.
January 1997	Israeli and Palestinian officials sign the Hebron agreement, in which Israel agrees to withdraw its forces from most of the West Bank city of Hebron and to resume Israeli military redeployment throughout the West Bank.
February 1997	Netanyahu announces the beginning of massive construction of Israeli settlements in the West Bank. Violent clashes occur between Palestinian protestors and Israeli troops, stalling peace negotiations.
October 1997	Iraq orders U.S. members of the UN weapons-inspection team to leave the country and threatens to shoot down any U.S. spy planes used for inspections. The remaining UNSCOM team leaves Iraq in support of their U.S. colleagues. After Russian diplomats intervene, the inspectors are allowed to return in November.
January 1998	Iranian president Muhammad Khatami, a political moderate, invites the U.S. to engage in a cultural dialogue and exchange with Iran.
August 7, 1998	U.S. embassies in Nairobi, Kenya, and Dar es Salaam, Tanzania, are simultaneously bombed, killing 257 and injuring thousands. Investigators suspect Osama bin Laden, a Saudi Arabian dissident said to be residing in Afghanistan. Bin Laden is also possibly linked to the 1993 World Trade Center bombing and bombings in Riyadh, Saudi Arabia.
August 22, 1998	The U.S. launches military strikes on suspected terrorist-related facilities in Afghanistan and Sudan in retaliation for the August 7 embassy bombings.
October 1998	At the Wye River Conference Center in Maryland, U.S., Israeli, and Arab leaders sign the Wye Memorandum, in which Israel grants Palestinians more control over the West Bank in exchange for guarantees of security and antiterrorism measures from Palestinian authorities.
December 1998	The Palestinian National Council revokes clauses in its founding charter that call for Israel's destruction.

December 15, 1998	In response to repeated Iraqi threats to suspend cooperation with UN weapons inspectors, the U.S. launches four days of air strikes on Iraq. At the end of the operation, Saddam Hussein permanently terminates cooperation with weapons inspectors.
February 7, 1999	King Hussein of Jordan dies. His son, Abdullah, takes the throne.
May 1999	Ehud Barak is elected prime minister of Israel.
October 1999	Saudi women attend the session of the Consultative Council, an advisory body of the Saudi Arabian government, for the first time.
May 2000	Israel withdraws its troops from southern Lebanon.
June 2000	Syrian president Hafiz al-Assad dies and is succeeded by his son, Bashar.
August 2000	Yasser Arafat and Ehud Barak, meeting with U.S. president Bill Clinton at Camp David, Maryland, try to negotiate a final peace settlement, but talks break down over the status of Jerusalem.
September 28, 2000	Israeli Parliament member Ariel Sharon visits a Jerusalem site holy to both Jews and Muslims with a 1,000-member armed guard. Palestinians respond with violence, sparking a new *intifada*.
October 12, 2000	A suicide terrorist attack damages the American naval ship USS *Cole* off the coast of Yemen and kills seventeen.
January 21–27, 2001	Peace negotiations between Israelis and Palestinians take place at the resort town of Taba, Egypt. Prime minister Barak calls off the talks on the eve of Israeli elections without any official agreements being reached.
February 2001	Ariel Sharon is elected prime minister of Israel.
February 15, 2001	The United States and Great Britain carry out bomb attacks aimed at Iraq's air defense network. The bombings have little international support.
April 2001	Iran and Saudi Arabia sign a major security accord to combat terrorism, drug trafficking and organized crime.
April 30, 2001	The Mitchell Commission, an American group headed by former senator George Mitchell, releases its report on the Israeli/Palestinian conflict. The document, calling for a cease-fire as well as a monitoring mechanism to watch over the growth of Israeli settlements and Israeli enclosures of Palestinians, becomes the basis for repeated new calls for peace.

September 11, 2001	Terrorists crash American jet planes into the World Trade Center in New York and the Pentagon in Washington, D.C. It is later discovered that the terrorists were all from Saudi Arabia and other Middle East nations.
October 2001	The Israeli tourism minister is killed by Palestinian terrorists. Citing the inadequate response of the Palestine National Authority, Israeli troops enter and occupy Palestinian areas in the West Bank.
January 5, 2002	Israel captures a Palestinian ship loaded with fifty tons of missiles, rockets, and other munitions off its coast; it accuses the Palestinian Authority of purchasing these weapons from Iran.
January 29, 2002	Two Middle East nations, Iran and Iraq, are named by President George W. Bush as part of an "axis of evil" for supporting terrorism and pursuing weapons of mass destruction.
March 9, 2002	Eleven Israelis are killed at the Moment Café in Jerusalem by a suicide bomber.
March 27, 2002	Twenty-eight Jews are killed at a Passover seder in Netanya by a suicide bomber.
March 29–May 2, 2002	In an effort to restore calm and prevent further violence, Sharon orders tanks into the West Bank. Israeli forces barricade Yasser Arafat in his government compound in Ramallah. Tanks level much of the compound, but stop short of taking Arafat captive. After over a month, the siege ends, and tanks withdraw from the West Bank. A UN investigation into the reported massacre of Palestinian noncombatants in a Jenin refugee camp is abandoned after Israel refuses to cooperate.
April 2002	Egypt, responding to Israel's crackdown on Arafat, downgrades its relations with Israel.
April 2, 2002	More than 200 Palestinian militants and bystanders take refuge in the Church of the Nativity in Bethlehem in order to escape Israeli military incursions in the West Bank. After five weeks of negotiations, the captives are allowed to leave the church; 13 of the gunmen are sent into exile, and 26 are handed over to Palestinian authorities.
June 2002	President George W. Bush calls for Israeli withdrawal and Palestinian statehood, pending reforms and new political leadership in the PNA. Israel reoccupies the entire West Bank except for the city of Jericho.

September 2002	Iran begins construction of its first nuclear reactor with Russian technical help over the objections of the United States.
September 12, 2002	President George W. Bush addresses the United Nations and calls on that body to enforce its disarmament resolutions against Iraq.
September 24, 2000	The United Nations Security Council passes a resolution that calls on Israel to withdraw from Palestinian towns.
November 8, 2002	Resolution 1441, which gives Iraq a final chance to disarm or face "serious consequences," is passed unanimously by the United Nations Security Council.
December 7, 2002	Iraq submits documentation required by UN Resolution 1441 in which it claims it disposed of all weapons of mass destruction.
January 2003	Elections return Israel's prime minister Ariel Sharon to power.
February–March 2003	Israel launches military incursions into Gaza in response to terrorist attacks.
March 7, 2003	UN chief inspector Hans Blix submits report to UN Security Council stating that Iraq has partially but not completely cooperated in weapons disarmament.
March 10, 2003	The PLO's central council, meeting in Ramallah, approves Arafat's proposal to name Abu Mazen as the PNA's new prime minister, and condemns violence against civilians.
March 14, 2003	President George W. Bush unveils a "road map" to peace that would result in the creation of a Palestinian state on land held by Israel by 2005.
March 18, 2003	In a televised address, President Bush gives Saddam Hussein 48 hours to leave Iraq or face invasion.
March 20, 2003	An American-led coalition begins military action against Iraq.

Organizations and Websites

The editors have compiled the following list of organizations concerned with the issues debated in this book. The descriptions are derived from materials provided by the organizations. All have publications or information available for interested readers. The list was compiled on the date of publication of the present volume; the information provided here may change. Be aware that many organizations take several weeks or longer to respond to inquiries, so allow as much time as possible.

American-Israeli Cooperative Enterprise (AICE)
2810 Blaine Dr., Chevy Chase, MD 20815
(301) 565-3918 • fax: (301) 587-9056
e-mail: mgbard@aol.com • website: www.us-israel.org

AICE seeks to strengthen the U.S.-Israel relationship by emphasizing values the two nations have in common and developing cooperative social and educational programs that address shared domestic problems. It also works to enhance Israel's image by publicizing novel Israeli solutions to these problems. It publishes the book *Partners for Change: How U.S.-Israel Cooperation Can Benefit America*. Its website includes the Jewish Virtual Library, a comprehensive online encyclopedia of Jewish history.

American Jewish Committee (AJC)
PO Box 705, New York, NY 10150
(212) 751-4000 • fax: (212) 838-2120
e-mail: PR@ajc.org • website: www.ajc.org

AJC works to strengthen U.S.-Israel relations, build international support for Israel, and support the Israeli-Arab peace process. The committee's numerous publications include the *AJC Journal*, the report *Muslim Anti-Semitism: A Clear and Present Danger*, and the papers "Iran and the Palestinian War Against Israel" and "The Arab Campaign to Destroy Israel."

Americans for Middle East Understanding (AMEU)
475 Riverside Dr., Room 245, New York, NY 10115-0245
(212) 870-2053 • fax: (212) 870-2050
e-mail: info@ameu.org • website: www.ameu.org

AMEU's purpose is to foster a better understanding in America of the history, goals, and values of Middle Eastern cultures and peoples, the rights of Palestinians, and the forces shaping U.S. policy in the Middle East. AMEU publishes *The Link*, a bimonthly newsletter, as well as books and pamphlets on the Middle East.

Center for Middle Eastern Studies
University of Texas, Austin, TX 78712
(512) 471-3881 • fax: (512) 471-7834
e-mail: cmes@menic.texas.edu
website: http://menic.utexas.edu/menic/cmes

The center was established by the U.S. Department of Education to promote a better understanding of the Middle East. It provides research and instructional materials, and publishes three series of books on the Middle East: the Modern Middle East Series, the Middle East Monograph Series, and the Modern Middle East Literatures in Translation Series.

Foundation for Middle East Peace
1763 N St. NW, Washington, DC 20036
(202) 835-3650 • fax: (202) 835-3651
e-mail: info@fmep.org • website: www.fmep.org

The foundation assists the peaceful resolution of the Israeli-Palestinian conflict by making financial grants available within the Arab and Jewish communities. It publishes the bimonthly *Report on Israeli Settlements in the Occupied Territories* and additional books and papers.

Institute for Palestine Studies (IPS)
3501 M St. NW, Washington, DC 20007
(202) 342-3990 • fax: (202) 342-3927
e-mail: ips@ipsjps.org • website: www.ipsjps.org

The Institute for Palestine Studies is a private, nonprofit, pro-Arab institute unaffiliated with any political organization or government. Established in 1963 in Beirut, the institute promotes research, analysis, and documentation of the Arab-Israeli conflict and its resolution. IPS publishes quarterlies in three languages and maintains offices all over the world. In addition to editing the *Journal of Palestine Studies*, the institute's U.S. branch publishes books and documents on the Arab-Israeli conflict and Palestinian affairs.

Jordan Information Bureau
2319 Wyoming Ave. NW, Washington, DC 20008
(202) 265-1606 • fax: (202) 667-0777
e-mail: JordanInfo@aol.com
website: www.jordanembassyus.org/new/jib/indexjib.shtml

The bureau provides political, cultural, and economic information on Jordan. It publishes fact sheets, speeches by Jordanian officials, and government documents, many of which are available on its website.

Middle East Forum

1500 Walnut St., Suite 1050, Philadelphia, PA 19102
(215) 546-5406 • fax: (215) 546-5409
e-mail: info@meforum.org • website: www.meforum.org

The Middle East Forum is a think tank that works to define and promote American interests in the Middle East. It supports strong American ties with Israel, Turkey, and other democracies as they emerge. It publishes the *Middle East Quarterly*, a policy-oriented journal. Its website includes articles, summaries of activities, and a discussion forum.

Middle East Institute

1761 N St. NW, Washington, DC 20036-2882
(202) 785-1141 • fax: (202) 331-8861
e-mail: mideasti@mideasti.org
website: www.themiddleeastinstitute.org

The institute's charter mission is to promote better understanding of Middle Eastern cultures, languages, religions, and politics. It publishes numerous books, papers, audiotapes, and videos as well as the quarterly *Middle East Journal*. It also maintains an Educational Outreach Department to give teachers and students of all grade levels advice on resources.

Middle East Media Research Institute (MEMRI)

PO Box 27837, Washington, DC 20038-7837
(202) 955-9070 • fax: (202) 955-9077
e-mail: memri@memri.org • website: www.memri.org

MEMRI translates and disseminates articles and commentaries from Middle East media sources and provides analysis on the political, ideological, intellectual, social, cultural, and religious trends in the region.

Middle East Policy Council

1730 M St. NW, Suite 512, Washington, DC 20036-4505
(202) 296-6767 • fax: (202) 296-5791
e-mail: info@mepc.org • website: www.mepc.org

The Middle East Policy Council was founded in 1981 to expand public discussion and understanding of issues affecting U.S. policy in the Middle East. The council is a nonprofit educational organization that operates nationwide. It publishes the quarterly *Middle East Policy Journal*.

Middle East Research and Information Project (MERIP)
1500 Massachusetts Ave. NW, Washington, DC 20005
(202) 223-3677 • fax: (202) 223-3604
website: www.merip.org

MERIP is a nonprofit, nongovernmental organization with no links to any religious, educational, or political organizations in the United States or elsewhere. Its mission is to educate the public about the contemporary Middle East with particular emphasis on U.S. foreign policy, human rights, and social justice issues. It publishes the bimonthly *Middle East Report.*

United States Department of State, Bureau of Near Eastern Affairs
U.S. Department of State
2201 C St. NW, Washington, DC 20520
(202) 647-4000
website: www.state.gov/p/nea

The bureau deals with U.S. foreign policy and U.S. relations with the countries in the Middle East and North Africa. Its website offers country information as well as news briefings and press statements on U.S. foreign policy.

Washington Institute for Near East Policy
1828 L St. NW, Suite 1050, Washington, DC 20036
(202) 452-0650 • fax: (202) 223-5364
e-mail: info@washingtoninstitute.org
website: www.washingtoninstitute.org

The institute is an independent, nonprofit research organization that provides information and analysis on the Middle East and U.S. policy in the region. It publishes numerous books, periodic monographs, and reports on regional politics, security, and economics, including *PeaceWatch*, which focuses on the Arab-Israeli peace process, and the reports *Democracy and Arab Political Culture* and *Radical Middle East States and U.S. Policy.*

Websites

Bitterlemons.org
www.bitterlemons.org

This website presents Israeli and Palestinian viewpoints on the Palestinian-Israeli conflict and peace process as well as related regional issues of concern.

Ha'Aretz Online
www.haaretzdaily.com

This is an online edition of one of the leading Israeli newspapers published in English.

Islamic Republic News Agency
www.irna.com

This agency of the government of Iran provides links to news articles and current affairs about that nation and the Middle East.

MidEastWeb
www.mideastweb.org

MidEastWeb is a website founded by people from different nations who are active in peace education efforts. Its website features articles and opinions about events in the region, as well as maps and a history of the conflict in the Middle East.

Saudi Arabia Ministry of Information
www.saudinf.com

This official Saudi government site has links to thousands of pages of information on the Kingdom of Saudi Arabia.

Bibliography of Books

Lila Abu-Lughod, ed.   *Feminism and Modernity in the Middle East.* Princeton, NJ: Princeton University Press, 1998.

Gilbert Achcar   *The Clash of Barbarisms: September 11 and the Making of the New World Disorder.* New York: Monthly Review Press, 2002.

Karen Armstrong   *Jerusalem: One City, Three Faiths.* New York: Knopf, 1996.

Naseer Aruri, ed.   *Palestinian Refugees: The Right of Return.* London, UK: Pluto, 2001.

Christiane Bird   *Neither East nor West: One Woman's Journey Through the Islamic Republic of Iran.* New York: Pocket Books, 2001.

Yossef Bodansky   *The High Cost of Peace: How Washington's Middle East Policy Left America Vulnerable to Terrorism.* Roseville, CA: Prima, 2002.

Daniel Brumberg   *Reinventing Khomeini: The Struggle for Reform in Iran.* Chicago: University of Chicago Press, 2001.

Roane Carey, ed.   *The New Intifada: Resisting Israel's Apartheid.* New York: Verso, 2001.

Noam Chomsky   *The Fateful Triangle: The United States, Israel and the Palestinians.* London, UK: Pluto Press, 2000.

Toby Dodge and   *Iraq at the Crossroads: State and Society in the Shadow of Regime Change.* New York: Oxford University Press, 2003.
Steven Simon, eds.

John L. Esposito and   *Islam and Democracy.* New York: Oxford University Press, 1996.
John O. Voll, eds.

Norman G. Finkelstein *Image and Reality of the Israel-Palestine Conflict.* New York: Verso, 2001.

Deborah J. Gerner, ed. *Understanding the Contemporary Middle East.* Boulder, CO: Lynne Reinner, 2000.

Victor Davis Hanson   *An Autumn of War: What America Learned from September 11 and the War on Terrorism.* New York: Anchor, 2002.

Birthe Hanssen   *Unipolarity and the Middle East.* Richmond, Surrey, UK: Curzon, 2000.

Nathanial Harris   *Israel and Arab Nations in Conflict.* New York: Raintree/SteckVaughan, 1999.

Dilip Hiro   *Iraq: In the Eye of the Storm.* New York: Thunder's Mouth Press, 2002.

Dilip Hiro — *Neighbors, Not Friends: Iraq and Iran After the Gulf Wars.* New York: Routledge, 2001.

Laurel Holliday — *Children of Israel, Children of Palestine: Our Own True Stories.* New York: Pocket Books, 1999.

Albert Hourani — *A History of the Arab Peoples.* Boston: Harvard University Press, 1997.

Mehran Kamrava — *Democracy in the Balance: Culture and Society in the Middle East.* Chappaqua, NY: Chatham House, 1998.

Martin Kramer — *Ivory Towers on Sand.* Washington, DC: Washington Institute for Near East Policy, 2001.

Walter Laqueur and Barry Rubin, eds. — *The Israel-Arab Reader: A Documentary History of the Middle East Conflict.* New York: Penguin USA, 2001.

David W. Lesch, ed. — *The Middle East and the United States: A Historical and Political Reassessment.* Boulder, CO: Westview Press, 2003.

Bernard Lewis — *The Middle East: A Brief History of the Last 2000 Years.* New York: Scribner, 1996.

Bernard Lewis — *What Went Wrong: The Clash Between Islam and Modernity in the Middle East.* New York: Harperperennial, 2003.

Philip Mattar, ed. — *The Encyclopedia of the Palestinians.* New York: Facts On File, 2000.

Mahmood Monshipouri — *Islamism, Secularism, and Human Rights in the Middle East.* Boulder, CO: Lynne Rienner, 1998.

Benny Morris — *Righteous Victims: A History of the Zionist-Arab Conflict, 1881–2001.* New York: Vintage, 2001.

Michael B. Owen — *Six Days of War: June 1967 and the Making of the Modern Middle East.* Novato, CA: Presidio, 2003.

Kenneth M. Pollack — *The Threatening Storm: The Case for Invading Iraq.* New York: Random House, 2002.

Milan Rai — *War Plan Iraq: Ten Reasons Against War with Iraq.* New York: Verso, 2002.

Edward W. Said — *The End of the Peace Process: Oslo and After.* New York: Vintage, 2000.

Elaine Sciolino — *Persian Mirrors: The Elusive Face of Iran.* New York: Free Press, 2000.

David K. Shipler — *Arab and Jew: Wounded Spirits in a Promised Land.* New York: Penguin, 2002.

Avi Shlaim

The Iron Wall: Israel and the Arab World. New York: W.W. Norton, 2001.

Charles D. Smith

Palestine and the Arab-Israeli Conflict. New York: Bedford/St. Martin's, 2000.

Shibley Telhami

The Stakes: America and the Middle East. Boulder, CO: Westview, 2002.

Harlan Ullman

Unfinished Business: Afghanistan, the Middle East and Beyond—Defusing the Dangers That Threaten American Security. New York: Citadel Press, 2002.

Index

in supply of, 130
U.S. addiction to, 130–31, 135–36
Oslo process, 99, 143
Ottaway, Marina, 119
Ottoman Empire, 13

Pakistan, 115
Palestine
number of Jews in, 18
partitioning of, 18, 35–36
Palestine Authority (PA), 143
Palestine Liberation Organization
(PLO), 40–41, 143
Palestine National Council, 146
Palestinians
are not persecuted under Israeli
occupation, 37
constitution of, 162–63
fence separating Israelis from,
166–68
illusion of security with, 170–71
is ineffective, 172–73
Palestinian view on, 172
pursuing negotiations instead of,
173–74
sacrifices negotiation positions,
171–72
nationhood for, rejection of, 36–37
Partnership for a New Generation
of Vehicles, 137
Payne, Henry, 134
Pearlman, Wendy, 161
Peretz, Martin, 157

Rabbo, Yasir Abed, 171
Rabin, Yitzhak, 143
refugees, Palestinian, 18, 147

Saudi Arabia, 59, 130
Seitz, Charmaine, 53
September 11 terrorist attacks, 47, 61
Sharon, Ariel
peace process and, 106, 149, 152
visit of, to Al-Aqsa mosque,
163–64
Sh'i' Da'wa Party, 79
Shi'i movements, 78–79
Shiites, 67
Six-Day war, 41, 67
Society of Muslim Brethren, 74–75
suicide bombings, 43, 79, 166–67
Syrian Arab Republic, 52

Takeyh, Ray, 60
Tenet, George, 105

terrorism
Israeli-Palestinian conflict and, 23,
155–56
Israeli-Palestinian peace process
and, 42–43, 152–53, 157–58
Arafat's condemnation of, 148
Tracinski, Robert, 150
Turkey, 52

United Nations
Development Programme
(UNDP), 58
partitioning of Palestine and, 18,
35–36
Security Council Resolution 242,
21, 24, 36
Security Council Resolution 446,
22
Security Council Resolution 465,
22
United States
aid to the Middle East, 94
energy conservation and, 131–33
Israeli-Palestinian peace process
and, 155, 156
Middle East resentment of, 110–11
military involvement in the Middle
East, 94
oil addiction of, 130–31, 135–36
reasons for interest in the Middle
East, 94–95
resistance to foreign control by,
15–16
role in Israeli-Palestinian conflict
expectations vs. reality for,
105–106
necessary intervention and,
101–102
resisting interventionist urge for,
106–107
role in Iraq, conflicting opinion
on, 109
see also democracy, U.S. promotion
of

violence
following Oslo peace agreements,
143
following Sharon's Al-Aqsa
mosque visit, 163–64
Iranian Islamic Revolution and,
78–79
Islamic fundamentalism fosters,
70–80
con, 81–91